THE ORIGINAL
BREAD MACHINE
COOKBOOK

SIMPLE HANDS-OFF RECIPES TO MAKE
DELICIOUS HOMEMADE LOAVES WITH ANY BREAD MAKER

INCLUDES GLUTEN-FREE RECIPES

TABLE OF CONTENT

INTRODUCTION
BAKING MADE EASY

TAKE A BREATH, CAN YOU FEEL IT?

A bread machine allows you to make bread in a precise shape, which is much faster and more convenient compared to traditional bread making methods. It is also much more convenient than traditional baking, as it eliminates the need for mixing or kneading. In order to produce good, fresh bread, it is important to use the best ingredients and quantities. If you choose to use a bread maker, it will be much easier to achieve consistent results by following a recipe and adjusting the settings accordingly. Many bread machines can also prepare dough, and some advanced models even have the capability to bake cakes.

HOW TO BAKE USING A BREAD MACHINE: THE ADVANTAGES/BENEFITS

Baking bread with a bread machine is less time consuming than regular bread making. It is much easier to create the recipe, and it is much more efficient. The specific model you own could have settings slightly different than others, but usually those settings will allow you to control the bread in the making with ease and making the final result very customizable to satisfy every palate.

As an experienced traditional baker I can tell you that using everyday a bread machine is much better than making bread by hand, especially for those who are not used to get their hands dirty and do not hav much time. The taste of homemade bread can be unpredictable; sometimes it can turn out too firm or overly soft. Furthermore, making bread in large quantities is ideal for big households, companies, or schools. With a bread machine, you can make a wide variety of breads, from basic to unusual. Baking a large batch of bread ensures that your family will have plenty for several days. Every two weeks, I make sure to have plenty of the type that everyone in my family enjoys. Finally, it's great for our finances: baking bread at home is not expensive compared to buying it from the store.

BREAD MACHINE CYCLES EXPLAINED

The bread machine bread making process consists of 5 automatic cycles; each will help your bread taste delicious. The preheat cycle assists the bread machine in heating and preheating, and it takes about 15 minutes to heat up. The kneading cycle kneads the bread, and it usually lasts for around 8 minutes. The rise cycle helps the bread rise before the baking cycle and takes around 25 minutes. During the punch cycle, the dough is kneaded again; this time softer, to release the gas bubble due to the fermentation of the yeast. Finally, the baking cycle bakes the bread, and it lasts for around 30 minutes. That's how bread is done.

HOW TO CHOOSE THE CORRECT BREAD MACHINE SETTINGS?

Among all the steps, this one is crucial. In the world of homemade bread baking, you are well on your way once you have completed the initial experiments and they have been successful. In that instance, if you want consistently excellent bread, attempt these methods. Gathering the right components for the bread recipe should be your first order of business. You should use the bread machine with its cycles, and only use the manual mode if required. If you've used the bread maker before to produce the same recipe, it will remember the settings. The kneading and baking cycles may be adjusted to fit your chosen settings if necessary. Now, without further ado, let's go more in-depth and discover many mouthwatering bread recipes.

BREAD ESSENTIALS
FLOUR, YEAST, WATER & SALT

The combination of simple ingredients is the foundation of bread making, but it is essential to have a thorough understanding of these ingredients to achieve a desirable outcome.

To begin, let's discuss flour. It is a vast subject, but for the sake of simplicity, it can be defined as the result of grinding a cereal, seed, or tuber. The most commonly used flours for baking include wheat flour (which has many varieties), oats, corn, rye, barley, and even nuts such as chestnut. Since wheat flour is the most frequently used, we will focus on it, although we will not delve into its varieties at this time.

In general terms, wheat flour is composed of starch and other elements, such as minerals, vitamins, proteins, and ashes, in varying proportions. The sifting of the milling process influences these factors. Whole grain flours, which retain the bran, differ from white flours, which have had the bran removed. There are also soft wheat and durum wheat flours, which vary in their protein content and, as a result, produce different bread outcomes.

The proteins (gliadin and glutenin) in the flour are responsible for the dough's formation and elasticity, which, along with fermentation, give the bread volume and consistency. As the flour is hydrated, the proteins bind, transforming into gluten. Manipulating the dough and oxygenating causes the dough to become elastic and workable. If the dough is well hydrated and kneaded, a protein mesh (glutinous network) forms and covers it. The more protein the flour has, the more water it will need, so it is important to be mindful of not adding too much water.

Yeast is the second major component of bread. Typically, a fungus suitable for consumption is used and can be found in two forms: dry or fresh. Keep in mind that fresh yeast is a living organism, so it must be properly stored as it loses strength over time. If dry yeast is used, the proportion should be one-third of the amount called for in the recipe for fresh yeast. For example, if the recipe calls for 10 grams of fresh yeast, you should use 3 grams of dry yeast.

Another way to make bread is through natural sourdough, the oldest method of fermenting bread (through bacteria present in the environment). Bread made with sourdough typically has a slightly acidic taste, lasts longer, has an intense aroma, and facilitates digestion due to bacterial fermentation. Making sourdough is straightforward, but it takes time (usually around five days).

Water and salt are simple ingredients with no significant complications or secrets. In fact, in professional bakeries, tap water is often used. Salt adds flavor and can be used in various forms, such as marine salt or salt with herbs. Bread does not have to have salt; it's up to the baker's tastes.

To sum up, the four main ingredients for bread dough—flour, yeast, water, and salt—must undergo the two crucial processes of kneading and fermentation in order to produce high-quality bread. Just a friendly reminder that not all breads require baking or a long period of kneading in the dough. Instead of using the oven, you may make bread in a skillet, griddle, casserole, or even steam it for a healthier alternative. Pita bread, Moroccan bread, North African bread, and other flatbreads are just a few of the numerous bread varieties that may be made in skillets.

YOUR FIRST LOAF

Your first loaf of bread. The smell rising from the perfectly browned crust is amazing. So fresh, so clean. It fills the room with the aroma of a summer day. The slightly charred crust, the texture of a brownie, sugar and flours that you sprinkled on top, each fold in the dough, all of your hard work, finally paying off. You cut the bread with a blunt knife, watching the sides of the slices curl inwards. Each bite brings a sense of accomplishment, as you savor the flavors of whatever you added to the dough. It is now perfect, that first loaf of homemade bread. It is perfect, this initial slice of bread, after staying in the oven for hours, waiting for you to come home from work and rest. Your next loaf of bread. No matter what you do, you cannot seem to replicate the first. You go through the motions, attempting to draw out the process in hopes of getting your first loaf, but the same thing always unravels. You want to throw in the towel. You can't continue to attempt this every week. Until you do something out of the ordinary. Until you throw that extra ingredient in. Letting your imagination roam and restlessly calling the dough to come to life, knowing what it needs to become something new, something better. That loaf of bread, just like your first, is amazing. You just need to give it a little more time when you bake. ***Picture of an artwork you've crafted.***

The next loaf of bread, it's the same hollow feeling in your chest, the same lethargy as you sat through the hours of proofing, the same feeling you get after trying, and the same pain after not getting the result you wanted. It is a negative feeling, a recurring feeling of defeat, the exact opposite of what you felt when you first baked that first loaf of bread. The next loaf of bread is hard to make, you put yourself through the motions as you added ingredients, trying to patch the problems with your initial formula. There waiting for your perfect loaf. It is never perfect.

I'm just starting out and honestly afraid that my failure will taste as bland as it looks, what with the unbaked, tight-textured, and likely flavorless crust. But no, there's no backing out now. I've got to go for it and I have full faith in you, dear bread. I just want to give you such a warm welcome to the world. What brought us together was a love for good bread. I began baking the loaf with my gut telling me that I'd love bread more than I do now, even if it means my heart would be longing for you every day. I can only feel this way because you, my bread, are truly good. This is the only bread I've ever eaten that makes me want to eat another piece right after I've finished the previous one. It's got to be that wonderful, I think.

I love its simplicity, I love its soft, smooth dough, and I love its melt-in-your's-mouth, down-to-the-last-crumb crust, making it one of the most addicting treats I've ever eaten. I love how its crust reflects the golden color of my loaf, giving it a delicate, yet rich texture. And then there's that scent. Oh, how I love your scent. I'm so fond of it because it reminds me of home and because it is so inviting. I love everything about you.

You are truly my bread-maker. I hope that you will be a good bread-maker. Here where I am, you are my first loaf. So why are you my last? Is it because I've concluded that the best-tasting bread ever is this loaf itself, and that after this, no other bread could ever be worthy of my heart again? Or is it simply the realization that I've outgrown the art of baking? Whatever it may be, thank you, bread. I guess I'll just have to go out and find my next one.

HOW TO STORE YOUR BREAD

Storing your bread is fairly simple and can be done anytime you make your bread. Store the items in the freezer or anywhere in your refrigerator. Sandwich loaves should be sliced before freezing. You can always just take out what you can eat, and store the rest for later in your refrigerator. Cooling your loaves after baking is very essential if you plan on freezing the bread; make sure it has completed its cool down cycle. Slice and add it to freezer bags

Remove all of the excessive air.

Bread machine bread is so delicious, you might create more than you, your family, and your friends can eat in one sitting. Here are some tips for storing your bread machine creations:

Dough. After the kneading cycle, remove the dough from the machine. If you plan on using the dough within three days, you can store it in the refrigerator. Form the dough into a disk and place it in a sealable freezer bag, or store the dough in a lightly oiled bowl covered with plastic wrap. Yeast action will not stop in the refrigerator, so punch the dough down until it is completely chilled, and then once a day. When you are ready to bake bread, remove the dough from the refrigerator, shape it, let it rise, and bake. Because bread machine dough contains no preservatives, you should freeze it if you aren't going to bake it within three days. Form the dough into a disk and place it in a sealable freezer bag. You can freeze bread dough for up to a month. When you are ready to bake the bread, remove the dough from the freezer, store it in the refrigerator overnight, shape it, let it rise, and bake. Before refrigerating or freezing the dough, you can shape it into braids, loaves, knots, or other shapes. Wrap the shapes tightly and store in the refrigerator (if you are baking within 24 hours) or the freezer. At the right time, unwrap the dough, allow it to rise at room temperature, and bake it.

Baked Bread. Once your baked bread is cooled, wrap the loaf in plastic wrap or a freezer bag and place it in the refrigerator or freezer. I suggest you to keep your baked bread

in the freezer for up to 6 months. To thaw the bread, remove it from the freezer, unwrap the loaf partially, and let it sit at room temperature. If you want to serve warm bread after refrigerating or freezing a loaf, wrap the bread in aluminum foil, and bake it in an oven preheated to 300°F for 10 to 15 minutes. Try not to believe that homemade bread should keep insofar as commercially made assortments. In our home, newly cooked bread is probably not going to keep going long at any rate. Thus, when it has cooled totally, I store it in a bread canister in the kitchen. Specialists keep up that the ideal approach to store bread is to wrap it firmly in foil or seal it in a plastic pack and keep it at room temperature. Continuously oppose the impulse to refrigerate bread on the grounds that staling is at it's generally fast in normal cooler temperatures.

If you truly need to keep bread for longer than a day or two, the ideal route is to freeze it. Except for extremely dried up loaves, most crisp bread can be solidified for around about a month wrapped and fixed in freezer packs. At the point when you need to eat it, enable the bread to defrost (still in its sack) at room temperature or defrost it on an exceptionally low force in the microwave. If you utilize just limited quantities of bread, it is a smart thought to cut bread before freezing and takes it out a couple of pieces one after another. Now that you have all this wonderful homemade bread, how can you store it to keep it fresh? Believe it or not, freezing your bread is the best option. Bread can be stored up to 2 months in a freezer, and warned up as needed. If you are planning on eating your bread soon after baking, leaving it out uncovered is one way to go. Even if the crust gets a little hard the inside should be fine.

An old-fashioned way to keep bread around longer is storing it in a bread box. This way the bread is covered and unexposed to air. Bread can also be wrapped in plastic to preserve it, just ensure that it's placed in a cool, dry area with no moisture. Whatever you decide to do, do not put fresh bread in the refrigerator, because it will become dried out. We do not want to waste every single piece of bread we made, we want to share them to others, and have it 'til supper and whatnot. Therefore, do not let your bread goes out of freshness, store bread properly, always follow the guidelines. Enjoy your baking.

TIPS & TRICKS TO BECOME A PRO

WHY WATER TEMPERATURE MATTERS

More than any other type of cooking, baking is a science and every detail matters. Your bread maker takes care of a lot of the science of baking bread, but there are still a few important factors under your control that will determine how successfully your bread turns out. The ingredient which determines how well your bread rises, and thus how well it turns out, is yeast. Because yeast is a living organism, it only does its job correctly under certain specific conditions.

This is why water temperature is so important. If the water is too cold the yeast will be sluggish, and it won't produce enough carbon dioxide. This will lead to loaves that don't raise enough, and have a dense, doughy consistency. If your water is too warm, it will kill the yeast, and this often leads to even less rising. In order to get the best results, you will want to use a kitchen thermometer and make sure your water is between 115°F and 125°F. Water heated to within this range provides the perfect environment for the yeast to activate and do its job. Also, be sure to keep track of how old your yeast is. Because it is a living organism, it will eventually die and won't be able to produce carbon dioxide. All yeast packages have an expiration date. If your yeast has passed, or is even close to, that date, throw it away and buy some fresh yeast.

SELECTING THE RIGHT KIND OF YEAST

There are many different types of yeast out there and choosing the correct one can be a challenge. Yeast is a naturally occurring organism, and it is the main ingredient used by bread makers to make leavened bread. Prior to the discovery of yeast, all bread was flatbread. The best type of yeast to use for most applications with your bread maker is quick-rise yeast. This differs from traditional active dry yeast because it activates even faster and produces carbon dioxide at a faster rate. In general, most of the yeast you will use to make bread with your bread maker will be dry yeast; however, there is one type of bread which gets its signature flavor from a wet type of yeast: sourdough. Sourdough is the oldest form of leavened bread and it is made using a wet "starter," rather than powdered yeast. You can make your own starter at home or purchase dry starter and hydrate it and feed it to keep it active.

BREAD FLOUR VS. ALL-PURPOSE FLOUR

Just like there are different types of yeast, there are different types of flour that will produce different types of bread. In general, it is recommended to use bread flour when baking in your bread maker, but depending on what type of loaf you want to make, this is not always the case. Bread flour is higher in protein than all-purpose flour, and as a result, bread made with bread flour has a higher gluten content. This will result in loaves that are chewier and denser than bread made with all-purpose flour. So, if you are trying to make a chewy French loaf, bread flour is certainly the way to go. However, a classic white bread or brioche may be lighter and fluffier with all-purpose flour.

SO...

-Your water has to be between 115°F and 125°F.
- Keep track of how old your yeast is.
- The best type of yeast is quick-rise yeast.
- All-purpose flour gives you lighter & fuffier results.

WEIGHT VS. VOLUME

In most cooking, using volume as a measure is perfectly fine, however, because baking is more of an exact science, the best way to get perfect results is by using weight to measure your ingredients, rather than volume. Over the years, bakers narrowed their measurements down to exact weights rather than volumes. However, because not everyone has easy access to scales, those weights were converted to volumes because more people had things handy like measuring spoons and cups. If you want to maximize your results, invest in a simple kitchen scale and follow the directions for weight rather than volume. If you do not want to use a kitchen scale, just be sure to use quality measuring utensils. Many cheaper measuring cups or spoons are not accurate, and this may negatively affect your final product.

MASTER THE MOISTURE IN YOUR DOUGH

In order to get the very best results when making bread, it is important to make sure your dough has the correct moisture content. This will affect how well the bread rises and how evenly it cooks. Traditionally, bakers have kneaded bread dough by hand and it was easy to keep track of how moist the dough was at any given time. Because your bread maker does all of the kneading for you, you won't have as much contact with the dough, but that doesn't mean that you can't inspect it to make sure it has the proper moisture. During the kneading cycle, check the dough. If it is soggy and not holding together, add some flour until the consistency becomes more firm. You should also add a little flour if the dough feels sticky to the touch or if dough comes off on your fingers when you touch it. Conversely, if the dough feels flaky or floury to the touch, add a little water until it becomes smooth and elastic.

How to tell if the dough is perfect: Poke it with your finger. Ideally, your dough should bounce back quickly when you poke it.

EXPERIMENTING WITH FLOURS

In addition to bread flour and all-purpose flour, you can also experiment with whole wheat flour, which will result in a dense yet nutty flavor that is a great source of nutrition.

By experimenting with different ratios of whole wheat to bread flour you can customize the perfect level of whole wheat, from just a slight hint to a very dense and nutritious loaf. You can also buy rye flour for mixing with either all-purpose or bread flour, for a hearty and tangy rye bread. The addition of a tablespoon of caraway seeds will give you a really authentic, deli-style rye bread. Since there are such a wide variety of different flours on the market now, you can experiment with adding many different types of flour.

We recommend adding small amounts of nut flour like almond flour for an extra hint of flavor.

SO...

- Invest in a simple kitchen scale.
- Make sure your dough has the correct moisture content.
- Check the dough during the kneading cycle.
- Experiment with different kinds of flours for various results.

MAKE PASTA WITH YOUR BREAD MAKER

While you won't be baking the pasta in the bread maker, you can take advantage of its powerful motor to take a lot of the effort out of making fresh pasta. Because pasta dough needs extensive kneading to come out smooth and even, you can place all of your pasta dough ingredients (flour, eggs, salt, and a bit of olive oil) into the baking pan and use the dough/pasta function to knead your dough to perfection effortlessly. When it is finished kneading, remove the dough from the machine and wrap in plastic wrap. Place the dough on a countertop and allow resting for about a half an hour. This will give the ingredients time to incorporate before you roll it and cut it fully.

ADDING INGREDIENTS TO YOUR BREAD

Once your bread maker has combined your bread ingredients, you will have an opportunity to add different ingredients to your bread dough. Chopped nuts and dried fruit make an excellent addition and will impart an interesting flavor and texture to your bread. You can also try adding things like chopped olives and fresh herbs, for earthy and delicious loaves that work wonderfully as a base for a sandwich or as a wholesome snack. Another fun way to add ingredients to your bread is by making sweet bread like cinnamon raisin or cranberry orange. Simply sprinkle in a bit of cinnamon mixed with sugar and a handful or raisins, or add dried cranberries with a teaspoon of fresh orange zest. Once you get started using your bread maker you will find that the possibilities for amazing, healthy, and creative bread are nearly limitless!

SO...

- Invest in a simple kitchen scale.
- Make sure your dough has the correct moisture content.
- Check the dough during the kneading cycle.
- Experiment with different kinds of flours for various results.

LET'S START YOUR BAKING MASTER CLASS

FRENCH BAGUETTE

Dough Recipes

1h 10min   *2 hours*   *1 ½ lb*

INGREDIENTS

1 cup and 2 tablespoons water

¾ teaspoon granulated sugar

1 ½ teaspoons salt

3 cups bread flour

2 tablespoons wheat germ

1 ¾ active dry yeast

Cornmeal

HOW TO MAKE IT

Add water, sugar, salt, bread flour, wheat germ and yeast to the bread pan.

Place the bread pan into the bread machine. Press "prog". Choose "dough program". Press "start". After the cycle has been complete, take the dough out of the machine.

Transfer to your kitchen table. Cover with plastic and rest for 10 minutes. Divide it into 2 portions.

Form a baguette from the 2 portions. Dust your baking pan with cornmeal.

Place the baguette on top of the baking pan. Cover with plastic. Let rise for 40 minutes.

Create slashes on top of the dough. Reheat your oven to 426 degrees F. Position a bowl of hot water on the bottom oven rack. Add the baking pan with baguette dough on the top rack. Bake for 30 minutes.

NUTRITION

Kcal: 386 kcal
Protein: 13.14 g
Fat: 2.06 g
Carbs: 76.86 g

CHEESE BREADSTICKS

Dough Recipes

 50 minutes   *2 hours*   *30 sticks*

INGREDIENTS

3 cup olive oil

¾ cup water

½ teaspoon granulated sugar

1 ½ teaspoons salt

1 cup sharp cheddar cheese, shredded

3 cups bread flour

1 teaspoon paprika

2 ¼ teaspoons active dry yeast

1 tablespoon olive oil

HOW TO MAKE IT

Pour olive oil and water into the bread pan. Add sugar, salt, cheese, flour, paprika and yeast to the pan.
Set pan into the bread machine.

Press "prog" and pick "dough program", hit "press" button.

Once cycle is complete, move the dough to a surface that has been fluffed. Squish the dough together. Cover baking pan with parchment paper.

Roll out the dough to form a rectangle. Slice the dough to form sticks. Place sticks on the baking pan.
Cover with plastic and let rest for 30 minutes.

Preheat your own to 375 degrees F. and brush top of the breadsticks with remaining oil. Bake the breadsticks for 20 minutes.

NUTRITION

Kcal: 491 kcal
Protein: 3.55 g
Fat: 44.62 g
Carbs: 20.29 g

PIZZA DOUGH

Dough Recipes

30 minutes   2h 10 minutes   1 ½ lb. dough

INGREDIENTS

Dough

1 cup water

1 teaspoon honey

1 ½ teaspoons salt

1 ½ tablespoons olive oil

2 2/3 cups bread flour

½ cup whole-wheat flour

1 ¾ teaspoons active dry yeast

Pizza

1 cup pizza sauce

Your favorite toppings

1 cup mozzarella cheese

NUTRITION

Kcal: 898
Protein: 42.38 g
Fat: 20.89 g
Carbs: 134.71 g

HOW TO MAKE IT

Add all dough ingredients to the bread pan.

Set it into the bread maker and press "prog".

Choose "dough program", hit "start" button to begin the process of making the dough.

Once completed, roll out the dough and knead.

Place in a pizza pan. Spread with pizza sauce and top with chosen toppings. Sprinkle cheese on top.

Bake in the oven at 375 degrees F for 30 to 40 minutes.

HERB FOCACCIA

HERB FOCACCIA

Dough Recipes

1 hour   *1h 50min*   *1 12x8 inch bread*

INGREDIENTS

1 cup and 2 tablespoons water

2 tablespoons olive oil

2 ¼ teaspoons dried Italian herbs

1 ½ teaspoons salt

3 cups and 3 tablespoons bread

flour

1 ½ teaspoons active dry yeast

Greasing / dusting

Flour

Olive oil

Cornmeal

Topping

3 tablespoons olive oil

¼ cup fresh herbs, chopped

¾ teaspoon salt

¼ cup Parmesan cheese, grated

HOW TO MAKE IT

Add dough ingredients to the bread pan. Place bread pan in the bread machine.

Hit "prog" button. Choose "dough program". Press "start" to initiate dough making cycle.

Once completed, transfer dough to a surface dusted with flour. Punch down the dough.

Let it rest for 10 minutes.

Brush your baking pan with oil. Dust baking pan with cornmeal. Roll out the dough into the pan. Cover with plastic and let rest for 40 minutes.

Preheat your oven to 450 degrees F. Create indentations on the dough. Drizzle with oil and top with the herbs, salt and cheese.

Bake in the oven for 20 minutes.

NUTRITION

Kcal: 218
Protein: 6.46 g
Fat: 4.28 g
Carbs: 37.57 g

PRETZELS

Dough Recipes

1 hour | 1h 50min | 12 pretzels

INGREDIENTS

1 cup water

1 tablespoon brown sugar

2 teaspoons salt

3 ¼ cups bread flour

2 ¼ teaspoons active dry yeast

2 cups water

2 tablespoons baking soda

HOW TO MAKE IT

Pour 1 cup water into the bread pan. Add sugar, salt, flour and yeast to the pan. Place this in the bread machine.

Press "prog" button. Pick "dough program" and hit "start" button.

Cover baking pan with parchment paper. Remove dough from the pan. Transfer to a flour surface. Divide into 12 portions. Then roll each portion into a thin rope and twist to form a pretzel and place these on the baking pan. Cover with plastic wrap and let rest for 30 minutes.

In a bowl, mix 2 cups water with baking soda. Fill a pot with water. Place pot over high heat. Bring to a boil.

Preheat your oven to 425 degrees F. Dip pretzels one at a time into the boiling water for 1 minute and 30 seconds.

Flip and let soak for another 1 minute and 30 seconds. Place pretzels on a wire rack. Dip pretzels in the baking soda mixture. Place these on the baking pan.

Bake for 20 minutes.

NUTRITION

Kcal: 136
Protein: 4.75 g
Fat: 0.67 g
Carbs: 27.22 g

KALAMATA ROLLS

Dough Recipes

40 minutes   *1h 50min*   *12 rolls*

INGREDIENTS

½ cup milk

1 tablespoon olive oil

¼ cup water

½ teaspoon salt

1 tablespoon sugar

1 ½ cups whole-wheat flour

1 ½ cups bread flour

½ cup Kalamata olives, pitted and sliced

1 teaspoon Herbes de Provence

2 ¼ teaspoons active dry yeast

HOW TO MAKE IT

Pour milk, oil and water into the bread pan. Add the rest of the ingredients.

Set bread pan into the bread machine. Hit "prog" button. Choose "dough program". Press "start".

Once cycle is finished, take the dough out.

Roll out the dough and divide into 12 pieces and form a roll from each portion.

Cover with plastic and let rest for 30 minutes and preheat your oven to 350 degrees F.

Bake in the oven for 20 minutes.

NUTRITION

Kcal: 140
Protein: 4.7 g
Fat: 2.77 g
Carbs: 25.03 g

GARLIC & CHEESE KNOTS

Dough Recipes

50 minutes   *1h 50min*   *12 knots*

INGREDIENTS

Dough

1 cup water

1 ½ tablespoons olive oil

1 teaspoon salt

3 cups bread flour

¼ cup milk powder

2 tablespoons potato flakes

2 tablespoons cheddar, grated

2 teaspoons active dry yeast

2 teaspoons garlic powder

Seasoning

2 tablespoons butter

3 cloves garlic, minced

¼ teaspoon salt

½ tablespoon fresh oregano

½ tablespoon fresh parsley

HOW TO MAKE IT

Add dough ingredients to the bread pan. Place bread pan into the bread maker.

Press "prog" button. Choose "dough program". Press "start" to start the cycle of making the dough.

Transfer dough to a floured surface. Sprinkle with garlic powder. Divide dough into 12 portions and roll in to a rope and form a knot shape. Place in a baking pan. Cover with plastic wrap and let rest for 30 minutes.

Preheat your oven to 350 degrees F. Add butter to a pan over medium heat. Add garlic, salt and herbs.

Brush with the butter mixture & bake for 20 minutes.

NUTRITION

Kcal: 163
Protein: 4.57 g
Fat: 4.35 g
Carbs: 25.99 g

SWEET DOUGH

Dough Recipes

30 minutes   *1h 30min*   *1 ½ lb. dough*

INGREDIENTS

HOW TO MAKE IT

½ cup milk

1 tablespoon olive oil

¼ cup water

½ teaspoon salt

1 tablespoon sugar

1 ½ cups whole-wheat flour

1 ½ cups bread flour

½ cup Kalamata olives, pitted and sliced

1 teaspoon Herbes de Provence

2 ¼ teaspoons active dry yeast

Pour milk, oil and water into the bread pan. Add the rest of the ingredients.

Set bread pan into the bread machine. Hit "prog" button. Choose "dough program". Press "start".

Once cycle is finished, take the dough out.

Roll out the dough and divide into 12 pieces and form a roll from each portion.

Cover with plastic and let rest for 30 minutes and preheat your oven to 350 degrees F.

Bake in the oven for 20 minutes.

NUTRITION

Kcal: 294
Protein: 9.11 g
Fat: 9.8 g
Carbs: 41.49 g

CINNAMON ROLLS

- the original bread machine cookbook -

CINNAMON ROLLS

Dough Recipes

50 minutes *1h 50min* *16 rolls*

INGREDIENTS

Dough

½ cup milk

2 eggs

4 tablespoons butter, sliced into cubes

1/3 cup granulated sugar

¾ teaspoon salt

1 teaspoon vanilla extract

1/3 cup cornstarch

1 ¾ teaspoons active dry yeast

Filling

2 teaspoons ground cinnamon

¼ cup brown sugar

3 tablespoons granulated sugar

Brushing

1 tablespoon butter

HOW TO MAKE IT

Put dough ingredients in the bread pan.

Place the bread pan in the bread machine.

Press "prog" button. Choose "dough program". Press "start".

While waiting for the cycle to complete, mix the filling ingredients in a bowl.

Divide dough into 2 portions. Cover with plastic wrap and let rest for 10 minutes.

Spray your baking sheet with oil. Roll out the dough.

Brush with butter Top with cinnamon sugar. Roll up the dough. Pinch the sides to seal. Place in the baking pan. Cover with plastic wrap.

Let rest for 30 minutes. Preheat your oven to 350 degrees F.

Bake in the oven for 30 minutes.

NUTRITION

Kcal:185
Protein: 4.68 g
Fat: 5.52 g
Carbs: 28.93 g

HERB & CHEESE KNOTS

Dough Recipes

 50 minutes

 1h 50 min

 12 knots

INGREDIENTS

1 cup water

1 ½ tablespoons olive oil

1 teaspoon salt

3 cups bread flour

¼ cup milk powder

¼ cup Parmesan cheese, grated

1 teaspoon oregano, chopped

2 teaspoons active dry yeast

NUTRITION

Kcal: 150
Protein: 4.97 g
Fat: 2.89 g
Carbs: 25.46 g

HOW TO MAKE IT

Put all ingredients into the bread pan. Set bread pan into the bread machine.

Hit "prog" button. Select "dough program". Press "start" to initiate dough-making process.

Place dough on a floured surface and divide into 12 portions. Roll into a rope and form a knot from the rope. Put the knots on a baking sheet and cover with plastic wrap.

Let rest for 30 minutes.

Preheat your oven to 350 degrees F. and bake in the oven for 20 minutes.

ITALIAN BREAD

White Bread

2 hours   1h 30min   1 ½ lb. brioche

INGREDIENTS

3 cups unbleached all-purpose flour

1 tbsp. brown sugar

1 1/2 tsps. salt

1 1/8 cups warm water (110 degrees F/45 degrees C)

1 1/2 tbsps. olive oil

1 1/2 tsps. active dry yeast

1 egg

1 tbsp. water

1 tbsp. sesame seeds

1 tbsp. cornmeal

NUTRITION

Kcal: 147
Protein: 4.14 g
Fat: 2.06 g
Carbs: 25.86 g

HOW TO MAKE IT

Into the pan of bread machine, add all ingredients apart from cornmeal, sesame seeds, egg, and one tbsp. of water in the order endorsed by machine's manufacturer. Set the machine to the dough cycle.

Separate the dough into two parts and shape into loaves.

Drizzle cornmeal onto a greased baking sheet. Transfer the loaves onto the pan with the seam side down.

Use water to rub the top of the loaves and allow to rise for about 50 minutes until double.

Preheat the oven to 190 degrees C (375 degrees F).

Use egg wash to rub the loaves. Drizzle with sesame seeds.

Make four slits of around 1/4 inch deep across the top of log.

Put a pan containing hot water at the bottom of oven. Then bake bread for around 25 to 30 minutes or until turned golden in color.

To prepare a crusty bread, then bake bread in the afternoon and then place it into the oven once again for five minutes prior to your meal.

You will definitely have a very crusty bread and you will be surprised by how much better it will be when you heat in the final five minutes.

12

BUTTERMILK WHITE BREAD

White Bread

5 minutes *3h 5min* *12 servings*

NUTRITION

Kcal: 34
Protein: 1 g
Fat: 1 g
Carbs: 5.7 g

INGREDIENTS

1 1/8 cups water

3 tbsps. honey

1 tbsp. margarine

1 1/2 tsps. salt

3 cups bread flour

2 tsps. active dry yeast

4 tbsps. powdered buttermilk

HOW TO MAKE IT

Into the pan of bread machine, place the ingredients in the order suggested by the manufacturer.

Select medium crust and white bread settings.

When it is done, carefully remove the loaf from the machine and allow it to cool down for at least 1 hour. Slice, serve.

Tip: *Use less yeast during the hot and humid months on summer.*

13

HONEY WHITE BREAD

1 cup milk

3 tbsps. unsalted butter, melted

2 tbsps. honey

3 cups bread flour

3/4 tsp. salt

3/4 tsp. vitamin c powder

3/4 tsp. ground ginger

1 1/2 tsps. active dry yeast

Follow the order as directed in your bread machine manual on how to assemble the Ingredients.

Use the setting for Basic Bread cycle.

When it is done, carefully remove the loaf from the machine and allow it to cool down for at least 1 hour. Slice, serve.

NUTRITION   Kcal: 152, Protein: 4 g, Fat: 2 g, Carbs: 28 g

DR. MICHAEL'S YEASTED CORNBREAD

White Bread

2 hours　　*1h 30min*　　*1 ½ lb. brioche*

INGREDIENTS

3 1/2 cups bread flour

1/2 cup cornmeal

1 tsp. salt

3 tbsps. white sugar

3 tbsps. shortening

1 cup milk

1/8 cup water

1 egg

2 1/2 tsps. active dry yeast

HOW TO MAKE IT

In the bread machine pan, place ingredients as the way the manufacturer described.

Set the Basic or White Bread to start and then cool the bread by transferring it from the pan to a rack.

Store it by wrapping in foil.

NUTRITION

Kcal: 386
Protein: 13.14 g
Fat: 2.06 g
Carbs: 76.86 g

15

COTTAGE CHEESE BREAD

White Bread

 50 minutes   1h 50 min   12 knots

INGREDIENTS

1/2 cup water

1 cup cottage cheese

2 tbsps. margarine

1 egg

1 tbsp. white sugar

1/4 tsp. baking soda

1 tsp. salt

3 cups bread flour

2 1/2 tsps. active dry yeast

NUTRITION

Kcal: 171
Protein: 7.3 g
Fat: 3.6 g
Carbs: 26.8 g

HOW TO MAKE IT

Into the bread machine, place the ingredients according to the order recommended by manufacturer and then push the start button.

In case the dough looks too sticky, feel free to use up to half cup more bread flour.
Divide the dough into 12 portions. Roll and form a ball with each piece. Cover with plastic wrap & let rest for 30 minutes.

Preheat your oven to 350 degrees F. and bake in the oven for 20 minutes.

CINNAMON SWIRL BREAD

White Bread

2 hours *1h 30min* *1 ½ lb. brioche*

NUTRITION
Kcal: 386
Protein: 13.14 g
Fat: 2.06 g
Carbs: 76.86 g

INGREDIENTS

1 cup milk

2 eggs

1/4 cup butter

4 cups bread flour

1/4 cup white sugar

1 tsp. salt

1 1/2 tsps. active dry yeast

1/2 cup chopped walnuts

1/2 cup packed brown sugar

2 tsps. ground cinnamon

2 tbsps. softened butter, divided

2 tsps. sifted confectioners' sugar,

HOW TO MAKE IT

In the bread machine, put in the milk, eggs, 1/4 cup butter, bread flour, sugar, salt and yeast following the order of ingredients suggested by the manufacturer; choose the Dough setting on the machine and press the Start button.

Once the machine has finished the whole cycle, place the dough on a clean surface that is covered with flour and punch it down to deflate the dough. Allow the dough to sit for 10 minutes.
In a bowl, combine the cinnamon, walnuts and brown sugar together.

Separate the dough in half and flatten each half into a 14x9-inch rectangle. Put 1 tbsp. of softened butter evenly on top of each rectangular dough and top each dough evenly with half of the walnut mixture. Roll each filled rectangular dough up from the short ends of the dough; seal the seams by pinching the dough securely.

Coat two 9x5-inch loaf pans with oil. Place the filled loaf rolls into the greased loaf pans, seam sides down. Cover the dough and allow it to rise in volume for about 30 minutes until it is almost double in size.

Preheat the oven to 350°F (175°C).

Put the dough in the preheated oven and bake for about 30 minutes until it turns slightly golden brown in color and the bottom of the loaf creates a hollow sound when tapped. In case the loaves turn brown too fast, use an aluminum foil to loosely cover the loaves in the last 10 minutes of the baking process. Allow the bread to cool down in the loaf pan for 10 minutes before placing the loaf on wire racks to cool down completely. Dust the top of the loaves with 1 tsp. of confectioners' sugar.

GARLIC BREAD

White Bread

50 minutes	*1h 50 min*	*12 knots*

INGREDIENTS

1 3/8 cups water

3 tbsps. olive oil

1 tsp. minced garlic

4 cups bread flour

3 tbsps. white sugar

2 tsps. salt

1/4 cup grated Parmesan cheese

1 tsp. dried basil

1 tsp. garlic powder

3 tbsps. chopped fresh chives

1 tsp. ground black pepper

2 1/2 tsps. bread machine yeast

NUTRITION

Kcal: 150
Protein: 4.97 g
Fat: 2.89 g
Carbs: 25.46 g

HOW TO MAKE IT

Follow the order of putting the Ingredients into the pan of the bread machine recommended by the manufacturer.

Choose the Basic or the White Bread cycle on the machine and press the Start button.

Place dough on a floured surface and divide into 10 portions. Roll and form a ball with each piece. Put the buns on a baking sheet and cover with plastic wrap.

Let rest for 30 minutes.

Preheat your oven to 350 degrees F. and bake in the oven for 20 minutes.

GRANNY'S SPECIAL BREAD

White Bread

NUTRITION

Kcal: 46
Protein: 1.4 g
Fat: 1.9 g
Carbs: 6.5 g

 5 minutes   3h 5min   12 servings

INGREDIENTS

1 1/4 cups skim milk

1 cup crispy rice cereal

3 cups bread flour

2 tbsps. honey

1 1/4 tsps. salt

1 1/2 packages active dry yeast

2 tbsps. margarine

HOW TO MAKE IT

Into the bread machine pan, add the ingredients according to the order given by manufacturer.

Use BASIC or WHITE BREAD setting and then press the START button.

Transfer dough to a bowl and cover with plastic. let rest for 1 hour. Preheat your oven to 350 degrees and bake in the oven for 30 minutes.

LIGHT OAT BREAD

1 cup milk

3 tbsps. unsalted butter, melted

2 tbsps. honey

3 cups bread flour

3/4 tsp. salt

3/4 tsp. vitamin C powder

3/4 tsp. ground ginger

1 1/2 tsps. active dry yeast

Into the bread machine pan, place the ingredients in order suggested by the manufacturer.

Select the setting for BASIC BREAD cycle.

When it is done, carefully remove the loaf fron the brad machine, place it on a cooking rak and let il cool down for at least 1 hour before slicing and serving.

NUTRITION   Kcal: 152, Protein: 4 g, Fat: 2 g, Carbs: 28 g

GRANDMA'S ENGLISH MUFFIN BREAD

White Bread

 15 minutes   *3h 20 min*   *24 sevings*

INGREDIENTS

3 cups all-purpose flour

2 1/4 tsps. Active dry yeast

1/2 tbsp. white sugar

1 tsp. salt

1/8 tsp. baking powder

1 cup warm milk

1/4 cup water

NUTRITION

Kcal: 150
Protein: 4.97 g
Fat: 2.89 g
Carbs: 25.46 g

HOW TO MAKE IT

Into the bread machine pan, put the Ingredients according to the manufacturer's recommendations. Set the machine to the dough cycle.

Separate the dough into 2 unequal portions and then form into loaves. Put one portion in a 9 x 5 inch loaf pan and the other in a 7 x 3 inch loaf pan it's recommended to use non-stick pans although greased and floured normal pans will be enough.

Cover the pans and let the dough to rise until doubled in size.

Bake for about 15 minutes at 205 degrees C (400 degrees F). You may want to bake for longer to have a more browned and chewier crust.

HOMEMADE WONDERFUL BREAD

White Bread

2 hours   *1h 30min*   *1 ½ lb. brioche*

INGREDIENTS

2 1/2 tsps. active dry yeast

1/4 cup warm water (110 degrees F)

1 tbsp. white sugar

4 cups all-purpose flour

1/4 cup dry potato flakes

1/4 cup dry milk powder

2 tsps. salt

1/4 cup white sugar

2 tbsps. margarine

1 cup warm water (110 degrees)

NUTRITION

Kcal: 386
Protein: 13.14 g
Fat: 2.06 g
Carbs: 76.86 g

HOW TO MAKE IT

Prepare the yeast, 1/4 cup warm water and sugar to whisk and then let it sit in 15 minutes.

Take all Ingredients together with yeast mixture to put in the pan of bread machine according to the recommended order of manufacture.

Choose basic and light crust setting.

When it is done, carefully remove the loaf from the machine and allow it to cool down for at least 1 hour. Slice, serve.

PEASANT BREAD

White Bread

 5 minutes

 3h 5min

 12 servings

NUTRITION
Kcal: 147
Protein: 4.14 g
Fat: 2.06 g
Carbs: 25.86 g

INGREDIENTS

1 1/2 cups water

1 tbsp. white sugar

1 1/2 tsps. salt

3 1/2 cups bread flour

2 1/2 tsps. active dry yeast

HOW TO MAKE IT

n the bread machine pan, measure all Ingredients according to the manufacturer's directions.

Set the machine to LIGHT or MEDIUM CRUST cycle; Start the machine.

Tip: To make a crispier crust, choose the French cycle or after first rise, turn machine off and start the cycle over.

RON'S WHITE BREAD

1 cup water

1 extra large egg, beaten

2 tbsps. dry milk powder

1 tbsp. white sugar

2 tbsps. vegetable oil

1 1/2 tsps. salt

1 cup bread flour

2 cups all-purpose flour

1 1/4 tsps. active dry yeast

Add the Ingredients in the order recommended by the manufacturer.

Set the machine to the BASIC BREAD setting and normal crust.

When it is done, carefully remove the loaf from the brad machine and place it on a cooking rack.

Let il cool down for at least 1 hour before slicing and serving.

NUTRITION Kcal: 91, Protein: 3 g, Fat: 3 g, Carbs: 14 g

NO CORN CORNBREAD

Breakfast Bread

10 minutes   *10 minutes*   *8 servings*

INGREDIENTS

½ cup almond flour

¼ cup coconut flour

¼ tsp. salt

¼ tsp. baking soda

3 eggs

¼ cup unsalted butter

2 Tbsp. low-carb sweetener

½ cup coconut milk

NUTRITION

Kcal: 65
Protein: 2 g
Fat: 6 g
Carbs: 2 g

HOW TO MAKE IT

Soften the butter in a microwave & lightly beat the eggs. After you've incorporated the milk, butter, and eggs into the bread pan, add the other ingredients.

After inserting the bread pan into the bread maker, turn it on. Push the start button after entering the bread machine's settings (Sweet Quick Bread, Light Color, 1.5 lb).

Turn off the bread maker when the cornbread is done baking.

Set aside a wooden cutting board and take out the bread pan.

Remove the bread from the pan after 10 minutes of sitting in the bread pan.

The bread pan is going to be quite hot, so be sure to use oven mitts before removing it.

Transfer the cornbread to a cooling rack once it has been removed from the pan.

Cornbread is more prone to breaking or crumbling when cut into slices if allowed to cool for at least 60 minutes.

GARLIC CHEESE BREAD LOAF

Breakfast Bread

 10 minutes   *45 minutes*   *10 sevings*

INGREDIENTS

3 cups all-purpose flour

2 1/4 tsps. Active dry yeast

1/2 tbsp. white sugar

1 tsp. salt

1/8 tsp. baking powder

1 cup warm milk

1/4 cup water

NUTRITION

Kcal: 299
Protein: 11 g
Fat: 27 g
Carbs: 4 g

HOW TO MAKE IT

Into the bread machine pan, put the ingredients according to the manufacturer's recommendations. Set the machine to the dough cycle.

Separate the dough into 2 unequal portions and then form into loaves. Put one portion in a 9 x 5 inch loaf pan and the other in a 7 x 3 inch loaf pan it's recommended to use non-stick pans although greased and floured normal pans will be enough.

Cover the pans and let the dough to rise until doubled in size.

Bake for about 15 minutes at 205 degrees C (400 degrees F). You may want to bake for longer to have a more browned and chewier crust.

CARDAMOM BREAD

Breakfast Bread

15 minutes   *4 hours*   *12 servings*

INGREDIENTS

HOW TO MAKE IT

½ cup whole milk, unsweetened,
at 90°F

¼ cup applesauce, unsweetened

1 egg, at room temperature

¼ cup honey

1 teaspoon salt

1 teaspoon ground cardamom

2 ¾ cup bread flour

2 teaspoons bread machine yeast

NUTRITION

Kcal: 100
Protein: 3 g
Fat: 2.5 g
Carbs: 17 g

Gather all the ingredients for the bread and plug in the bread machine having the capacity of 1 ½ pounds of bread recipe.

Add all the ingredients into the bread bucket in the order mentioned in the ingredient list.
When adding yeast, make a small well in the center of the flour and add yeast in it; make sure it doesn't come in contact with wet ingredients, salt, and honey.

Shut the lid, press the "dough" button and then "start/stop" button to knead the ingredients until incorporated and thoroughly combined.

Then select the "basic/white" cycle setting and, if not available, press the up/down arrow button to adjust baking time according to your bread machine model; the baking will take 2 to 4 hours.

Then press the crust button to select light or medium crust if available, choose the right loaf size if available, and press the "start/stop" button to switch on the bread machine.

When the bread machine beeps, open the lid, take out the bread bucket by using oven mitts, loosen the side of the bread by using a non-stick spatula and lift out the bread by turning the pan over a clean surface.

Let the bread cool on a wire rack for 15 minutes, then cut it into twelve slices and serve.

WALNUT COCOA BREAD

Breakfast Bread

15 minutes   *3 hours*   *12 sevings*

NUTRITION

Kcal: 168
Protein: 5 g
Fat: 7 g
Carbs: 23 g

INGREDIENTS

2/3 cup milk

1/3 cup water

5 Tbsp. butter, softened

1/3 cup packed brown sugar

5 Tbsp. baking cocoa

1 tsp salt

3 cups bread flour

2¼ tsp active dry yeast

2/3 cup chopped walnuts, toasted

HOW TO MAKE IT

Add each ingredient except the walnuts to the bread machine in the order and at the temperature recommended by your bread machine manufacturer.

Close the lid; select the sweet loaf, low crust setting on your bread machine, and press start.

Just before the final kneading, add the walnuts.

When the bread machine has finished baking, remove the bread and put it on a cooling rack. Serve and enjoy!

28 ITALIAN SEMOLINA BREAD

1 cup water

1 teaspoon salt

2½ tablespoons butter

2½ teaspoons sugar

2¼ cups flour

1/3 cups semolina

1½ teaspoons dry yeast

Add all of the ingredients to your bread machine, carefully following the instructions of the manufacturer.

Set the program of your bread machine to Italian Bread/ Sandwich mode and set crust type to Medium. Press START.

Wait until the cycle completes. Once the loaf is ready, take the bucket out and let the loaf cool for 5 minutes. Gently shake the bucket to remove the loaf. Cool down and slice.

CHOCOLATE ZUCCHINI BREAD

Breakfast Bread

10 minutes   *50 minutes*   *10 sevings*

INGREDIENTS

2 cups grated zucchini, excess moisture removed

4 eggs

2 Tbsp. olive oil

1/3 cup low-carb sweetener

1 tsp. vanilla extract

1/3 cup coconut flour

¼ cup unsweetened cocoa powder

½ tsp. baking soda

½ tsp. salt

1/3 cup sugar-free chocolate chips

HOW TO MAKE IT

Add all of the ingredients to your bread machine, carefully following the instructions of the manufacturer

Set the program of your bread machine to Basic/White Bread and set crust type to Medium and Press START.

Wait until the cycle completes. Once the loaf is ready, take the bucket out and let the loaf cool for 5 minutes.

Gently shake the bucket to remove the loaf. Transfer to a cooling rack, slice and serve.

NUTRITION

Kcal: 149
Protein: 3 g
Fat: 8 g
Carbs: 7 g

30
CRISPY FRENCH BREAD DELIGHT

Breakfast Bread

10 minutes   3h 30min   9 sevings

NUTRITION
Kcal: 135
Protein: 3 g
Fat: 2 g
Carbs: 26 g

INGREDIENTS

2/3 cup water at 80 degrees F

2 teaspoons olive oil

1 tablespoon sugar

2/3 teaspoon salt

2 cups white bread flour

1 teaspoon instant yeast

HOW TO MAKE IT

Add all of the ingredients to your bread machine, carefully following the instructions of the manufacturer.

Set the program of your bread machine to French bread and set crust type to Light. Press START.

Once the cycle is completed and the loaf is ready, take the bucket out and let the loaf cool for 5 minutes.

Gently shake the bucket to remove the loaf and transfer to a cooling rack. Slice and serve.

31 HONEY-FLAVORED BREAD

2¼ cups white flour

¼ cup rye flour

1 cup water

1 whole egg, beaten

1 tablespoon vegetable oil

1 teaspoon salt

1½ tablespoons honey

1 teaspoon dry yeast

Incorporate all of the components into your bread maker in accordance with the manufacturer-recommended procedures.

Choose Basic/White Bread as the program and Medium as the crust type on your bread maker. Hit the start button. Be patient and let the cycle finish. Leave the loaf in the bucket to cool for 5 minutes after it's done baking.

Remove the bread by gently shaking the bucket. After transferring to a cooling rack, cut into serving pieces.

NUTRITION Kcal: 177, Protein: 6 g, Fat: 3 g, Carbs: 33 g

WAFFLES

Breakfast Bread

10 minutes   *5 minutes*   *10 waffles*

INGREDIENTS

100 g Strong flour

50 g plain flour

1.5 g salt

15 g sugar

15 g honey

115 g milk + 1 egg

4 g dry yeast

50 g soft room temperature butter

30 g Pearl or nibbed Sugar

NUTRITION

Kcal: 183
Protein: 12.14 g
Fat: 13.06 g
Carbs: 4.16 g

HOW TO MAKE IT

Preheat the waffle iron to medium heat.

Put ingredients within the bread machine pan. Put all of the ingredients into the bread machine. If your machine has a yeast container, pour the yeast into it. If not, add yeast as well. Select the BASIC dough course and press the start.

After the machine adds the dry yeast, wait for several minutes depending on the machine and add soft room temperature butter. When the dough course has finished, take out the pan. Add pearl sugar and mix well.

By using a spoon, scoop dough and put them on to perchement sheet or baking sheet, preferably non-stick sheet. Leave it about 20 mins until they become twice in size.

Carefully spoon or spatula-load them onto a preheated baking sheet and bake until golden. So that they may get crispy, let them cool.

33 HONEY BREAD WITH CREAM AND COCONUT MILK

Breakfast Bread

 20 minutes

 3h 30min

 8 sevings

NUTRITION

Kcal: 135
Protein: 3 g
Fat: 2 g
Carbs: 26 g

INGREDIENTS

3 ¾ cups almond flour

1 ¾ cups bran meal

1 ¼ cups cream

1/3 cup coconut milk

2 tablespoons honey

2 tablespoons vegetable oil

2 teaspoons dry yeast

2 teaspoons salt

HOW TO MAKE IT

Pour in the cream, coconut milk, ½ cup of water, honey, and vegetable oil.

Put in the flour and salt. Make a groove in the flour and put in the yeast.

Bake on the BASIC program. Once the loaf is ready, take the bucket out and let the bread cool for about one hour. Slice and serve.

34 MILK ALMOND BREAD

1 ¼ cups milk

5 ¼ cups almond flour

2 tablespoons butter

2 teaspoons dry yeast

1 tablespoon sugar

2 teaspoons salt

Pour the milk into the form and ½ cup of water. Add flour.

Put butter, sugar, and salt in different corners of the mold. Make a groove in the flour and put in the yeast.

Set your bread machine on on the BASIC program.

When it is done, crefully remove the loaf from the pan and let it cool down before slicing. Enjoy!

NUTRITION Kcal: 352, Protein: 10 g, Fat: 4 g, Carbs: 5 g

CHOCOLATE CHIP SCONES

Breakfast Bread

10 minutes   *15 minutes*   *8 scones*

INGREDIENTS

1 cup of milk

¾ cup of softened butter

1 egg

5 teaspoons of baking powder

½ teaspoon of salt

½ cup of sugar

3 cups of all-purpose flour

1 tablespoon of powdered sugar
for sprinkling on scones

NUTRITION

Kcal: 213
Protein: 7.97 g
Fat: 17.89 g
Carbs: 10.46 g

HOW TO MAKE IT

Preheat the oven to 400 degrees F (200 degrees C). and lightly grease a baking sheet.

Add the ingredients to the bread pan and select a setting that does not have a rising cycle like a pizza, pasta or cookie dough setting. If all you have is a basic dough setting, turn out the batter/dough before the rising cycle commences.

Pour onto a flour dusted surface and rollout until about ½ inch thick.Cut into about 8 to 12 wedges and place on the greased or buttered baking sheet.

Bake 15 minutes until golden brown. Remove and dust with powdered sugar if you like. Serve.

BASIC RYE BREAD

Rye Bread

15 minutes　　*3h 20 min*　　*24 sevings*

INGREDIENTS

1 1/8 cups warm water

2 tablespoons molasses

1 tablespoon vegetable oil

1 teaspoon salt

2 cups all-purpose flour

1 1/2 cups rye flour

3 tablespoons packed brown sugar

1 tablespoon unsweetened cocoa powder

3/4 teaspoon caraway seed

2 teaspoons bread machine yeast

HOW TO MAKE IT

Add ingredients according to bread machine's manufacturer's Directions.

Use the whole wheat and light crust settings.

Take out the bread from the machine and let it cool down for about an hour.

Slice the loaf and serve.

NUTRITION

Kcal: 386
Protein: 13.14 g
Fat: 2.06 g
Carbs: 76.86 g

PUMPERNICKEL BREAD

Rye Bread

2 hours | *1h 30min* | *1 ½ lb. brioche*

INGREDIENTS

1 1/8 cups warm water

1 1/2 tablespoons vegetable oil

1/3 cup molasses

3 tablespoons cocoa

1 tablespoon caraway seed

1 1/2 teaspoons salt

1 1/2 cups bread flour

1 cup rye flour

1 cup whole wheat flour

1 1/2 tablespoons vital wheat gluten (optional)

2 1/2 teaspoons bread machine yeast

HOW TO MAKE IT

Place ingredients in the pan of the bread machine in the order recommended by the manufacturer.

Select Basic cycle; press Start.

Take out the bread from the machine and let it cool down completely.

Slice the bread and serve.

NUTRITION

Kcal: 386
Protein: 13.14 g
Fat: 2.06 g
Carbs: 76.86 g

BUTTERMILK RYE BREAD

Rye Bread

45 minutes *30 minutes* *14 sevings*

INGREDIENTS

1 1/3 cups water

2 tablespoons vegetable oil

2 tablespoons honey

1 1/2 tablespoons vinegar

2 tablespoons powdered
buttermilk

2 1/3 cups bread flour

1 cup rye flour

1/3 cup dry potato flakes

1 teaspoon salt

2 teaspoons active dry yeast

1 teaspoon caraway seed

HOW TO MAKE IT

Place the ingredients into the pan of the bread machine in the order suggested by the manufacturer.

Select the Basic or White Bread setting, and Start.

Take out the bread from the machine and let it cool down for about an hour.

Slice the loaf and serve.

Tip: Enjoy at breakfast with butter and jam.

NUTRITION

Kcal: 386
Protein: 13.14 g
Fat: 2.06 g
Carbs: 76.86 g

CARAWAY RYE BREAD

Rye Bread

---

10 minutes   *4 hours*   *12 servings*

INGREDIENTS

1 1/4 cups lukewarm water

(100 degrees F/38 degrees C)

2 tablespoons dry milk powder

1 teaspoon salt

2 tablespoons brown sugar

2 tablespoons molasses

2 tablespoons butter

3/4 cup whole wheat flour

1 3/4 cups bread flour

3/4 cup rye flour

1 1/2 tablespoons caraway seeds

1 3/4 teaspoons active dry yeast

HOW TO MAKE IT

Put lukewarm water, milk powder, salt, brown sugar, molasses, butter.

Add whole wheat flour, bread flour, rye flour, caraway seeds, and yeast into the pan of a bread machine in the order suggested by the manufacturer.

Select the Grain setting and 2-pound loaf size.

Take out the bread from the machine and let it cool down completely.

Slice the bread and serve.

NUTRITION

Kcal: 386
Protein: 13.14 g
Fat: 2.06 g
Carbs: 76.86 g

CHAI CAKE

Rye Bread

15 minutes   *3 hours*   *10 sevings*

INGREDIENTS

1 (1.1 oz.) pkg chai tea powder

3/4 cup hot water

1/4 cup Chardonnay wine

1/2 teaspoon vanilla extract

1 egg yolk

1/2 cup frozen raspberries

1 tbsp butter, room temperature

1/2 cup bread flour

1/4 cup rye flour

1 cup all-purpose flour

1/2 cup wheat bran

1 (.25 ounce) pkg active dry yeast

1/2 cup coarsely chopped walnuts

1/2 teaspoon caraway seed

1/4 cup white sugar

1 teaspoon smoked salt flakes

HOW TO MAKE IT

Prepare the chai tea using one packet or two tablespoons of dry mix stirred into 3/4 cup hot water. Allow to cool for about 10 minutes.

Combine the chai tea, Chardonnay, vanilla extract, egg yolk, frozen raspberries, and butter in the pan of a bread machine. Bread, rye, all-purpose, wheat bran, yeast, walnuts, caraway seed, sugar, and salt should be added.

Push the Start button after choosing the "Sweet" option with the "Light Crust" topping. When the bread has finished baking, allow it to cool for at least 30 minutes before slicing and serving.

NUTRITION

Kcal: 386
Protein: 13.14 g
Fat: 2.06 g
Carbs: 76.86 g

DANISH RUGBROD RYE BREAD

Rye Bread

10 minutes *3 hours* *24 servings*

INGREDIENTS

1 1/2 cups water

1 tablespoon honey

1 tablespoon butter

1 teaspoon salt

2 cups rye flour

1 cup all-purpose flour

1 cup whole wheat flour

1/4 cup rye flakes (optional)

1 tablespoon white sugar

2 teaspoons bread machine yeast

NUTRITION

Kcal: 80
Protein: 13.14 g
Fat: 2.06 g
Carbs: 76.86 g

HOW TO MAKE IT

Put water, honey, butter, salt, rye flour, all-purpose flour, whole wheat flour, rye flakes, sugar, and yeast, respectively, into the pan of your bread machine.

Select Basic setting and press Start.

Take out the bread from the machine and let it cool down completely.

Slice the bread and serve.

DANISH SPICED RYE BREAD SIGTEBROD

Rye Bread

20 minutes   *35 minutes*   *16 sevings*

NUTRITION
Kcal: 386
Protein: 13.14 g
Fat: 2.06 g
Carbs: 76.86 g

INGREDIENTS

1 cup milk

1 cup water

3 tablespoons butter

1/2 cup light molasses

1/3 cup white sugar

1 tablespoon grated orange zest

1 tablespoon fennel seed

1 tablespoon anise seed

1 tablespoon caraway seed

1 tablespoon cardamom

1 teaspoon salt

2 (.25 ounce) pkg active dry yeast

1/4 cup warm water (110 degrees F/45 degrees C)

2 cups rye flour

5 cups all-purpose flour

3 tablespoons butter, melted

HOW TO MAKE IT

Heat milk in a medium saucepan until scalding and small bubbles are forming around the edges, but just before the milk reaches a boil.

Remove pan from heat and stir in the water, butter, molasses, sugar, orange zest, anise seed, caraway seed, cardamom and salt; allow to step and cool 30 minutes at room temperature.

In a bread maker, stir the yeast into the warm water and let sit for 5 minutes. Pour the cooled milk and spice mixture into the bread machine with the yeast mixture.

Add the flour to the bread machine. Run the bread machine on the dough cycle.

Grease two 9x5 inch loaf pans. When the dough cycle is complete, remove the dough from the machine, divide in half, form into 2 loaves, and place in the prepared loaf pans. Cover and allow to rise for 30 minutes, or until your finger leaves a small dent when you poke the loaves.

Preheat oven to 375 degrees F (190 degrees C).

After 35 to 40 minutes in the oven, check to see whether the loaves sound hollow when tapped on the bottom. Melt the butter and brush it over the heated loaves; let them cool before cutting..

EUROPEAN BLACK BREAD

Rye Bread

2 hours | *1h 30min* | *1 ½ lb. brioche*

INGREDIENTS

1 1/8 cups warm water

1 1/2 tablespoons vegetable oil

1/3 cup molasses

3 tablespoons cocoa

1 tablespoon caraway seed

1 1/2 teaspoons salt

1 1/2 cups bread flour

1 cup rye flour

1 cup whole wheat flour

1 1/2 tablespoons vital wheat gluten (optional)

2 1/2 teaspoons bread machine yeast

HOW TO MAKE IT

Place ingredients in the pan of the bread machine in the order recommended by the manufacturer.

Select Basic cycle; press Start.

Take out the bread from the machine and let it cool down completely.

Slice the bread and serve.

NUTRITION

Kcal: 386
Protein: 13.14 g
Fat: 2.06 g
Carbs: 76.86 g

HEALTH DYNAMICS RYE BREAD

Rye Bread

15 minutes　　*30 minutes*　　*12 sevings*

INGREDIENTS

2 eggs

3/4 cup warm water

2 tablespoons vegetable oil

2 tablespoons molasses

2 1/2 cups rye flour

1/4 cup cornstarch

2 teaspoons lecithin

1 1/4 teaspoons sea salt

3 teaspoons active dry yeast

NUTRITION

Kcal: 386
Protein: 13.14 g
Fat: 2.06 g
Carbs: 76.86 g

HOW TO MAKE IT

Place ingredients in the pan of the bread machine in the order recommended by the manufacturer.

Select Regular cycle and medium crust setting; press Start.

Take out the bread from the machine and let it cool down completely.

Slice your loaf, serve and enjoy!

Tip: While dough is mixing, check the consistency, it should be slightly sticky.

MONTANA RUSSIAN BLACK BREAD

Rye Bread

NUTRITION

Kcal: 386
Protein: 13.14 g
Fat: 2.06 g
Carbs: 76.86 g

 20 minutes   *45 minutes*   *10 servings*

INGREDIENTS

2 1/2 cups whole

wheat bread flour

1 cup rye flour

3 tablespoons cocoa powder

2 tablespoons bread flour

1 tablespoon wheat germ

1 tablespoon caraway seeds

2 teaspoons active dry yeast

1 cup flat warm porter beer

1/2 cup strong brewed coffee

2 tablespoons balsamic vinegar

2 tablespoons olive oil

2 tablespoons honey

1 tablespoon molasses

1 teaspoon sea salt

1/4 teaspoon onion powder

1 egg white

1 tablespoon warm water

HOW TO MAKE IT

In the order the manufacturer suggests, combine whole wheat bread flour, rye flour, cocoa powder, bread flour, molasses, caraway seeds, yeast, beer, coffee, vinegar, olive oil, honey, wheat germ, sea salt, and onion powder in a bread machine. Set bread machine for kneading cycle.

Line a baking sheet with parchment paper.

Remove dough from bread machine and shape into a rustic loaf on the prepared baking sheet. Make slits on top of loaf in crisscross formation. Let dough rise for 1 hour.

Preheat oven to 395 degrees F (202 degrees C).

Whisk egg white and warm water together in a small bowl. Drizzle the egg white mixture over the loaf's surface.

The bread needs 45 to 50 minutes in a preheated oven to be fully baked. Let the bread rest for at least an hour before cutting and serving.

CLASSIC GLUTEN-FREE BREAD

Gluten-Free Bread

5 minutes   *15 minutes*   *12 sevings*

INGREDIENTS	HOW TO MAKE IT

INGREDIENTS

½ cup butter, melted

3 tbsp. coconut oil, melted

6 eggs

2/3 cup sesame seed flour

1/3 cup coconut flour

2 tsp baking powder

1 tsp psyllium husks

½ tsp xanthan gum

½ tsp salt

HOW TO MAKE IT

Pour in eggs, melted butter, and melted coconut oil into your bread machine pan.

Add the remaining ingredients to the bread machine pan. Set bread machine to gluten-free.

When the bread is done, remove the bread machine pan from the bread machine.

Let cool slightly before transferring to a cooling rack.

You can store your bread for up to 3 days.

NUTRITION

Kcal: 146
Protein: 3.54 g
Fat: 14 g
Carbs: 1.3 g

GLUTEN-FREE CHOCOLATE ZUCCHINI BREAD

Gluten-Free Bread

 5 minutes

 15 minutes

 12 sevings

INGREDIENTS

1 ½ cups coconut flour

¼ cup unsweetened cocoa powder

½ cup erythritol

½ tsp cinnamon

1 tsp baking soda

1 tsp baking powder

¼ tsp salt

¼ cup coconut oil, melted

4 eggs

1 tsp vanilla

2 cups zucchini, shredded

NUTRITION

Kcal: 185
Protein: 5.14 g
Fat: 17.06 g
Carbs: 6.06 g

HOW TO MAKE IT

Shred the zucchini and use paper towels to drain excess water, set aside.

Lightly beat eggs with coconut oil then add to bread machine pan.

Add the remaining ingredients to the pan.
Set bread machine to gluten-free.

When the bread is done, remove the bread machine pan from the bread machine.

Let cool slightly before transferring to a cooling rack.

You can store your bread for up to 5 days.

HONEY OAT BREAD

Gluten-Free Bread

15 minutes   *3 hours*   *8 sevings*

INGREDIENTS

2 1/3 cups pure oat flour

(certified gluten-free oat flour)

1 cup pure rolled oats

2 ¼ teaspoons baking powder

1 ¼ teaspoons salt

1 teaspoon baking soda

1 egg

1 cup yogurt, plain

¾ cup almond milk

¼ cup of coconut oil

¼ cup honey

HOW TO MAKE IT

Add all wet ingredients first in the bread pan before the dry ingredients.

Press the "Basic" or "Normal" mode of the bread machine. Select "Medium" as the crust color setting.

Wait until the machine finishes the mixing, kneading, and baking cycles.

Take out the bread from the machine.

Let it cool down for about an hour before slicing.

NUTRITION

Kcal: 181
Protein: 7.04 g
Fat: 7 g
Carbs: 24.3 g

NUTTY CINNAMON BREAD

Gluten-Free Bread

 10 minutes   *2 hours*   *8 sevings*

INGREDIENTS

3 ½ cups gluten-free self-rising flour

½ cup pecans, chopped

¼ cup butter

3 tablespoons brown sugar

1 ½ tablespoons powdered milk

2 teaspoons cinnamon

1 teaspoon salt

1 ¼ cups water

HOW TO MAKE IT

Pour the water first into the bread pan, and then add the dry ingredients.

Select the "Normal" or "Basic" mode of the bread machine with the light crust color setting.

Allow the machine to complete all cycles. Remove the bread from the machine.

Cool down completely before slicing the bread.

NUTRITION

Kcal: 141
Protein: 3.14 g
Fat: 25.06 g
Carbs: 21.06 g

NISU BREAD

Gluten-Free Bread

10 minutes   *2 hours*   *8 sevings*

INGREDIENTS

4 cups gluten-free self-rising flour

½ cup of sugar

3 tablespoons butter

1 teaspoon ground cardamom

1 teaspoon salt

1 egg

1 cup evaporated milk

¼ cup of water

NUTRITION

Kcal: 184
Protein: 5.04 g
Fat: 27 g
Carbs: 31.3 g

HOW TO MAKE IT

Add the wet ingredients first to the bread pan before adding the dry ingredients.

Press the "Normal" or "Basic" mode and light crust setting on the bread machine.

Wait until every cycle is through.

Cooldown the bread completely before slicing and serving.

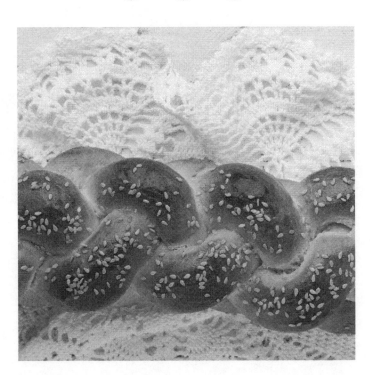

MAPLE SYRUP SPICE BREAD

Gluten-Free Bread

15 minutes   *3 hours*   *10 sevings*

INGREDIENTS

2 ½ cups gluten-free oat flour

½ cup raisins

¼ cup of sugar

1 tablespoon maple syrup

1 tablespoon cinnamon

1 tablespoon dried orange peel, minced

1 ½ teaspoons yeast

½ teaspoon nutmeg

¾ cup almond milk

3 tablespoons aquafaba

2 tablespoons vegetable oil

NUTRITION

Kcal: 168
Protein: 4 g
Fat: 3 g
Carbs: 30 g

HOW TO MAKE IT

Put all wet ingredients into the bread pan. Add the dry ingredients. Use the "Normal" or "Basic" mode and light crust color setting of your bread machine.

Wait until the cycles are over. Move the bread to a wire rack. Slice the bread once it has completely cooled down.

CHERRY-BLUEBERRY LOAF

Gluten-Free Bread

10 minutes   *3 hours*   *1 loaf*

INGREDIENTS

4 cups gluten-free oat flour

¼ cup brown sugar

1/3 cup dried cherries

1/3 cup dried blueberries

2 teaspoons yeast

1 ½ teaspoons salt

1 cup of water

2 tablespoons vegetable oil

HOW TO MAKE IT

After pouring the water and oil into the bread pan, add the dry ingredients into the mix.

Press the "Normal" or "Basic" mode of the bread machine. Choose either a light or medium crust color setting.

Once the cycles are done, transfer the bread to a wire rack. Cooldown the bread completely before slicing.

NUTRITION

Kcal: 181
Protein: 7.04 g
Fat: 7 g
Carbs: 24.3 g

GLUTEN-FREE LOAF

Gluten-Free Bread

5 minutes   *15 hours*   *12 sevings*

INGREDIENTS

½ cup butter, melted

3 tbsp. coconut oil, melted

2/3 cup sesame seed flour

1/3 cup coconut flour

2 tsp baking powder

1 tsp psyllium husks

½ tsp xanthan gum

½ tsp salt

6 eggs

HOW TO MAKE IT

Pour in eggs, melted butter, and melted coconut oil into your bread machine pan.

Add the remaining ingredients to the bread machine pan. Set bread machine to gluten-free.

When the bread is done, remove the bread machine pan from the bread machine.

Let cool slightly before transferring to a cooling rack.

You can store your bread for up to 3 days.

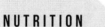

NUTRITION

Kcal: 141
Protein: 3.14 g
Fat: 25.06 g
Carbs: 21.06 g

HEALTHY GRAIN-FREE BAGELS

Gluten-Free Bread

10 minutes   20 minutes   6 servings

INGREDIENTS

1/4 cup sour cream

1 1/2 cups almond flour

3 eggs

NUTRITION

Kcal: 181
Protein: 7.04 g
Fat: 7 g
Carbs: 24.3 g

HOW TO MAKE IT

Preheat your oven to 350 degrees. Grease five wells with nonstick spray in a donut pan; set aside.

Beat eggs until creamy and light; stir in sour cream until very smooth. Mix in almond flour until well combined.

Spread the batter into the donut molds; bake for about 20 minutes. Let cook and slice to serve. Best served toasted with sour cream or butter.

CREAM OF ORANGE BREAD

Gluten-Free Bread

5 minutes   *15 hours*   *12 sevings*

INGREDIENTS

2 cups of rice flour

¾ cup potato flour

¼ cup tapioca flour

3 tablespoons sugar

2 tablespoons orange zest

1 tablespoon xanthan gum

2 ¼ teaspoons active dry yeast

1 teaspoon lemon zest, minced

1 teaspoon salt

¼ teaspoon cardamom

3 eggs

¾ cup milk, half-and-half

¾ cup of water

3 tablespoons vegetable oil

HOW TO MAKE IT

Add first the wet ingredients into the bread pan, then the dry ingredients.

Set the bread machine to "Basic", "Normal", or "White" mode.

Allow the machine to finish the mixing and baking cycles. Take out the pan from the machine.

Wait for 10 minutes before transferring the bread to a wire rack. When the bread has completely cooled down, slice it and serve.

NUTRITION

Kcal: 181
Protein: 7.04 g
Fat: 7 g
Carbs: 24.3 g

HEALTHY CELERY LOAF

Fruit and Vegetable Bread

2 h 40 min   *50 minutes*   *1 loaf*

INGREDIENTS

1 can (10 oz) cream of celery soup

3 tablespoons low-fat milk, heated

1 tablespoon vegetable oil

1¼ teaspoons celery salt

¾ cup celery, fresh/sliced thin

1 tablespoon celery leaves, chopped

1 whole egg

¼ teaspoon sugar

3 cups bread flour

¼ teaspoon ginger

½ cup quick-cooking oats

2 tablespoons gluten

2 teaspoons celery seeds

1 pack of active dry yeast

HOW TO MAKE IT

Add all of the ingredients to your bread machine, carefully following the instructions of the manufacturer.

Set the program of your bread machine to BASIC/WHITE Bread and set crust type to Medium.

Press START and wait until the cycle completes.

Once the loaf is ready, take the bucket out and let the loaf cool for 5 minutes.

Gently shake the bucket to remove the loaf. Transfer to a cooling rack, slice and serve.

NUTRITION

Kcal: 73
Protein: 3 g
Fat: 4 g
Carbs: 8 g

BROCCOLI AND CAULIFLOWER BREAD

Fruit and Vegetable Bread

5 minutes	*15 minutes*	*12 sevings*

INGREDIENTS

¼ cup water

4 tablespoons olive oil

1 egg white

1 teaspoon lemon juice

2/3 cup grated cheddar cheese

3 tablespoons green onion

½ cup broccoli, chopped

½ cup cauliflower, chopped

½ teaspoon lemon pepper

2 cups bread flour

1 teaspoon bread machine yeast

HOW TO MAKE IT

Add all of the ingredients to your bread machine, carefully following the instructions of the manufacturer.

Set the program of your bread machine to BASIC/WHITE Bread and set crust type to Medium.

Press START and wait until the cycle completes.

Once the loaf is ready, take the bucket out and let the loaf cool for 5 minutes.

Gently shake the bucket to remove the loaf and transfer to a cooling rack, slice and serve.

NUTRITION

Kcal: 156
Protein: 5 g
Fat: 8 g
Carbs: 17 g

ZUCCHINI HERBED BREAD

Fruit and Vegetable Bread

2 h 20 min   50 minutes   1 loaf

INGREDIENTS

½ cup water

2 teaspoon honey

1 tablespoons oil

¾ cup zucchini, grated

¾ cup whole wheat flour

2 cups bread flour

1 tablespoon fresh basil, chopped

2 teaspoon sesame seeds

1 teaspoon salt

1½ teaspoon active dry yeast

HOW TO MAKE IT

Add all of the ingredients to your bread machine, carefully following the instructions of the manufacturer.

Set the program of your bread machine to Basic/White Bread and set crust type to Medium.

Press START. Wait until the cycle completes.

Once the loaf is ready, take the bucket out and let the loaf cool for 5 minutes. Gently shake the bucket to remove the loaf and transfer to a cooling rack, slice and serve. Enjoy!

NUTRITION

Kcal: 153
Protein: 5 g
Fat: 1 g
Carbs: 28 g

POTATO BREAD

Fruit and Vegetable Bread

NUTRITION

Kcal: 35
Protein: 4 g
Fat: 1 g
Carbs: 19 g

 3 hours

 45 minutes

 2 loaves

INGREDIENTS

1 3/4 teaspoon active dry yeast

2 tablespoon dry milk

1/4 cup instant potato flakes

2 tablespoon sugar

4 cups bread flour

1 1/4 teaspoon salt

2 tablespoon butter

1 3/8 cups water

HOW TO MAKE IT

Put all the liquid ingredients in the pan. Add all the dry ingredients, except the yeast. Form a shallow hole in the middle of the dry ingredients and place the yeast.

Press down firmly on the pan within the machine and seal the top. Pick the default option and then pick the crust color you want. Hit the start button.

Before slicing, let the bread cool.

WALNUT FIG BREAD

1 tbsp sugar

1 tbsp salt

1.50 cups water

3 cups bread flour

1 cup rye flour

1 tbsp active dry yeast

2 cups chopped dried figs

1 cup chopped walnuts

Add the ingredients to the bread pan in the order indicated but reserve the figs and walnuts to add them later after the beep in the kneading cycle.

Select the White bread setting for a 2-pound loaf and medium crust.

When done, let it rest for 10 minutes and then slice and serve.

NUTRITION Kcal: 352, Protein: 10 g, Fat: 4 g, Carbs: 5 g

ONION POTATO BREAD

Fruit and Vegetable Bread

1 h 20 min   *45 minutes*   *2 loaves*

INGREDIENTS

2 tablespoon quick rise yeast

4 cups bread flour

1 1/2 teaspoon seasoned salt

3 tablespoon sugar

2/3 cup baked potatoes, mashed

1 1/2 cup onions, minced

2 large eggs

3 tablespoon oil

3/4 cup hot water
(115° F to 125°F)

HOW TO MAKE IT

Put the liquid ingredients in the pan. Add the dry ingredients, except the yeast.

Form a shallow well in the middle using your hand and put the yeast.

Place the pan in the machine, close the lid, turn it on and select the **EXPRESS BAKE** 80 setting and start the machine.

Once the bread is cooked, leave on a wire rack for 20 minutes or until cooled.

NUTRITION

Kcal: 160
Protein: 6 g
Fat: 2 g
Carbs: 44 g

CURD BREAD

Fruit and Vegetable Bread

4 hours   *15 minutes*   *12 sevings*

INGREDIENTS

¾ cup lukewarm water

3 2/3 cups wheat bread machine flour

¾ cup cottage cheese

2 Tablespoon softened butter

2 Tablespoon white sugar

1½ teaspoon sea salt

1½ Tablespoon sesame seeds

2 Tablespoon dried onions

1¼ teaspoon bread machine yeast

NUTRITION

Kcal: 156
Protein: 5 g
Fat: 8 g
Carbs: 17 g

HOW TO MAKE IT

Place all the dry and liquid ingredients in the pan and follow the instructions for your bread machine.

Pay particular attention to measuring the ingredients. Use a measuring cup, measuring spoon, and kitchen scales to do so.

Set the baking program to BASIC and the crust type to MEDIUM.

If the dough is too dense or too wet, adjust the amount of flour and liquid in the recipe.

When the program has ended, take the pan out of the bread machine and let cool for 5 minutes.

Shake the loaf out of the pan. If necessary, use a spatula and wrap the bread with a kitchen towel and set it aside for an hour. Otherwise, you can cool it on a wire rack.

CURVY CARROT BREAD

Fruit and Vegetable Bread

2 hours | 15 minutes | 12 servings

INGREDIENTS

¾ cup milk, lukewarm

3 tablespoons butter, melted at room temperature

1 tablespoon honey

¾ teaspoon ground nutmeg

½ teaspoon salt

1 ½ cups shredded carrot

3 cups white bread flour

2 ¼ teaspoons bread machine or active dry yeast

NUTRITION

Kcal: 142
Protein: 2.33 g
Fat: 0.8 g
Carbs: 32.2 g

HOW TO MAKE IT

Take 1 ½ pound size loaf pan and first add the liquid ingredients and then add the dry ingredients.

Place the loaf pan in the machine and close its top lid.

Plug the bread machine into power socket. For selecting a bread cycle, press "Quick Bread/Rapid Bread" and for selecting a crust type, press "Light" or "Medium". Start the machine and it will start preparing the bread.

After the bread loaf is completed, open the lid and take out the loaf pan. Allow the pan to cool down for 10-15 minutes on a wire rack. Gently shake the pan and remove the bread loaf.

Make slices and serve.

BEETROOT PRUNE BREAD

Fruit and Vegetable Bread

3 hours   *30 minutes*   *20 sevings*

INGREDIENTS

HOW TO MAKE IT

1½ cups lukewarm beet broth

5¼ cups all-purpose flour

1 cup beet puree

1 cup prunes, chopped

4 tablespoons extra virgin olive oil

2 tablespoons dry cream

1 tablespoon brown sugar

2 teaspoons active dry yeast

1 tablespoon whole milk

2 teaspoons sea salt

Prepare all of the ingredients for your bread and measuring means (a cup, a spoon, kitchen scales). Carefully measure the ingredients into the pan, except the prunes.

Place all of the ingredients into the bread bucket in the right order, following the manual for your bread machine. Close the cover.

Select the program of your bread machine to BASIC and choose the crust color to MEDIUM. Press START. After the signal, put the prunes to the dough. Wait until the program completes.

When done, take the bucket out and let it cool for 5-10 minutes. Shake the loaf from the pan and let cool for 30 minutes on a cooling rack. Slice, serve and enjoy the taste of fragrant homemade bread.

NUTRITION

Kcal: 443
Protein: 9.9 g
Fat: 8.2 g
Carbs: 81.1 g

ORANGE AND WALNUT BREAD

Grain, Seed and Nut Bread

2h 50min   *45 minutes*   *12 sevings*

INGREDIENTS

1 egg white

1 tablespoon water

½ cup warm whey

1 tablespoons yeast

4 tablespoons sugar

2 oranges, crushed

4 cups flour

1 teaspoon salt

1 and ½ tablespoon salt

3 teaspoons orange peel

1/3 teaspoon vanilla

3 tablespoons walnut and almonds

Crushed pepper, salt for garnish

HOW TO MAKE IT

Add all of the ingredients to your Bread Machine (except egg white, 1 tablespoon water and crushed pepper/ cheese).

Set the program to DOUGH cycle and let the cycle run.

Remove the dough (using lightly floured hands) and carefully place it on a floured surface. Cover with a light film/cling paper and let the dough rise for 10 minutes.

Divide the dough into thirds after it has risen and place on a lightly flour surface, roll each portion into 14x10 inch sized rectangles.

Use a sharp knife to cut carefully cut the dough into strips of ½ inch width. Pick 2-3 strips and twist them multiple times, making sure to press the ends together.

Preheat your oven to 400 degrees F. Take a bowl and stir egg white, water and brush onto the breadticks. Sprinkle salt, pepper & cheese.

Bake for 10-12 minutes until golden brown. Remove from baking sheet and transfer to cooling rack Serve and enjoy!

NUTRITION

Kcal: 156
Protein: 5 g
Fat: 8 g
Carbs: 17 g

BLUEBERRY BREAD

Fruit and Vegetable Bread

3h 15min   *45 minutes*   *1 loaf*

INGREDIENTS

1 1/8 to 1¼ cups Water

6 ounces Cream cheese, softened

2 tablespoons Butter or margarine

¼ cup Sugar

2 teaspoons Salt

4½ cups Bread flour

1½ teaspoons Grated lemon peel

2 teaspoons Cardamom

2 tablespoons Nonfat dry milk

2½ teaspoons Red star brand active dry yeast

2/3 cup dried blueberries

NUTRITION

Kcal: 180
Protein: 9 g
Fat: 3 g
Carbs: 250 g

HOW TO MAKE IT

Place all Ingredients except dried blueberries in bread pan, using the least amount of liquid listed in the recipe.

Select light crust setting and raisin/nut cycle. Press start. Observe the dough as it kneads.

After 5 to 10 minutes, if it appears dry and stiff or if your ma- chine sounds as if it's straining to knead it, add more liquid 1 tablespoon at a time until dough forms a smooth, soft, pliable ball that is slightly tacky to the touch.

At the beep, add the dried blueberries.

After the baking cycle ends, remove bread from pan, place on cake rack, and allow to cool 1 hour before slicing.

GOLDEN BANANA BREAD

Fruit and Vegetable Bread

1 h 40 min   *40/45 minutes*   *1 loaf*

INGREDIENTS

1 teaspoon Baking powder

1/2 teaspoon Baking soda

2 bananas, peeled and halved

2 cups all-purpose flour

2 eggs

3 tablespoon Vegetable oil

3/4 cup white sugar

NUTRITION

Kcal: 310
Protein: 3 g
Fat: 12 g
Carbs: 40 g

HOW TO MAKE IT

Put all the Ingredients in the bread pan. Select dough setting. Start and mix for about 3-5 minutes.

After 3-5 minutes, press stop. Do not continue to mix. Smooth out the top of the dough

Using the spatula and then select bake, start and bake for about 50 minutes. After 50 minutes, insert a toothpick into the top center to test doneness.

Test the loaf again. When the bread is completely baked, remove the pan from the machine and let the bread remain in the pan for 10 minutes.

Remove bread and cool in wire rack.

APRICOT & NUTS CAKE BREAD

Grain, Seed and Nut Bread

20 minutes   *4h 30min*   *8 servings*

INGREDIENTS

1 1/3 cups water

Two tablespoons butter softened

Three tablespoons honey

2/3 cups of bread flour

One teaspoon salt

One teaspoon active dry yeast

1 cup Dried apricots, snipped

1 cup chopped nuts

NUTRITION

Kcal: 73
Protein: 3 g
Fat: 4 g
Carbs: 8 g

HOW TO MAKE IT

Take a medium bowl, place apricots in it, pour in water, and let soak for 30 minutes.

Then remove apricots from the water, reserve the water, and chop apricots into pieces.

Gather the remaining ingredients needed for the bread. Power on bread machine that has about 2 pounds of the bread pan.

Put all the ingredients into the bread machine pan, except for apricots and nuts in the order mentioned in the ingredients list.

Press the "Bread" button, press the start button, let mixture knead for 5 minutes, add chopped apricots and nuts and continue kneading for 5 minutes until all the pieces have thoroughly combined and incorporated.

Select the "basic/white" cycle, press the up/down arrow to do baking to 4 hours, choose light or medium color for the crust, and press the start button. When the timer of the bread machine beeps, open the ma- chine.

It should come out spotless; else bake for another 10 to 15 minutes. Cut bread into eight slices and then serve.

CHERRY AND ALMOND BREAD

Grain, Seed and Nut Bread

10 minutes | 4 hour | 8 sevings

INGREDIENTS

1 1/3 Milk, lukewarm

2 tbsp Butter, unsalted, softened

3 tablespoons honey

2/3 cups of bread flour

1 teaspoon salt

1 teaspoon active dry yeast

1 cup Dried cherries

1 cup Slivered almonds, toasted

NUTRITION

Kcal: 156
Protein: 5 g
Fat: 8 g
Carbs: 17 g

HOW TO MAKE IT

Gather all the ingredients needed for the bread. Power on bread machine that has about 2 pounds of the bread pan.

Add all the ingredients in the order mentioned in the ingredients list into the bread machine pan.

Press the "Dough" button, key the left button, and let mixture knead for 5 to 10 minutes.

Then select the "basic/white" down arrow to set baking time to 4 hours, select light or medium color for the crust, and press the start button.

Then prudently lift out the bread and put it on a wire rack for 1 hour or more until cooled.

Cut bread into sixteen slices and then serve.

NUTTY WHEAT BREAD

Fruit and Vegetable Bread

10 minutes   *4 hours*   *12 servings*

INGREDIENTS

½ cup Water, lukewarm

1 tablespoon olive oil

4 cups Whole wheat flour

1 tsp Dry yeast, active

1 tbsp Brown sugar

1 tsp Salt

½ cup Chopped pecans

½ cup Chopped walnuts

NUTRITION

Kcal: 187
Protein: 5 g
Fat: 7 g
Carbs: 28 g

HOW TO MAKE IT

Add all the ingredients needed for the bread.

Power on bread machine that has about 2 pounds of the bread pan.

Add all the ingredients in the order listed in the ingredients list into the bread machine pan except for pecans and nuts.

Press the "Dough" switch, press the start button, let mixture knead for 5 minutes, add pecans and nuts, and then continue kneading for another 5 minutes until all the ingredients have thoroughly combined and incorporated.

Then select the "basic/white" cycle, press the up/down arrow to make the baking time to 4 hours.

Select light or medium color for the crust, and press the start button.

Then put the bread on a wire rack for 1 hour or more until cooled and cut bread into twelve slices and then serve.

HAZELNUT YEAST BREAD

Fruit and Vegetable Bread

10 minutes   *3 hours*   *16 servings*

INGREDIENTS

1 1/3 Milk, lukewarm

2 tbsp Butter, unsalted, softened

3 tablespoons honey

2/3 cups of bread flour

1 teaspoon salt

1 tso Almond extract

1 teaspoon active dry yeast

1 cup Dried cranberries

1 Egg

1 cup Chopped hazelnuts, toasted

HOW TO MAKE IT

Place all the ingredients needed for the bread.

Then power on bread machine that has about 2 pounds of the bread pan.

Add all the ingredients in the order stated in the ingredients list into the bread machine pan except for nuts.

Press the "Dough" button, press the start button, let mixture knead for 5 minutes, add nuts, and then knead for another 5 minutes until all the ingredients have thoroughly combined and incorporated.

Then select the "basic/white" cycle, or press the up/down arrow to set baking time to 3 hours.

Select light or medium color for the crust, and then press the start button.

Put it on a wire rack for 1 hour or more until cooled. Cut bread into sixteen slices and then serve.

NUTRITION

Kcal: 139
Protein: 5 g
Fat: 6 g
Carbs: 18 g

DATE-NUT YEAST BREAD

Grain, Seed and Nut Bread

10 minutes   *4 hours*   *12 servings*

INGREDIENTS

½ cup Water, lukewarm

1 tablespoon vegetable oil

4 cups almond flour

1 tsp Dry yeast, active

1 tbsp Brown sugar

1 tsp Salt

1 cup Dates, chopped

½ cup Walnuts, chopped

HOW TO MAKE IT

Gather all the ingredients needed for the bread and power on bread machine that has about 2 pounds of the bread pan.

Add all the ingredients in the order cited in the ingredients list into the bread machine pan.

Press the "Dough" button, push the start button.

Allow the mixture to knead for 5 to 10 minutes until all the pieces have been thoroughly combined and incorporated. Select the "basic/white" cycle, or press the up/down arrow to set baking day to 4 hours.

Select light or medium color for the crust, and then press the start button.

Then handover it to a wire rack for one hour or more until cooled. Cut bread into twelve slices and then serve.

NUTRITION

Kcal: 123
Protein: 4 g
Fat: 2 g
Carbs: 24 g

WALNUT BREAD WITH DRY YEAST

Grain, Seed and Nut Bread

10 minutes　　　*4 hour*　　　*12 sevings*

INGREDIENTS

1/2 cup Water, lukewarm

2 Egg, at room temperature

1 tbsp Butter, unsalted, softened

4 cups Bread flour

1 tsp Dry yeast, active

1/2 cup milk, nonfat

1 tsp Salt

1 cup Chopped walnuts, toasted

NUTRITION

Kcal: 135
Protein: 5 g
Fat: 5 g
Carbs: 19 g

HOW TO MAKE IT

Add all the ingredients needed for the bread & power on bread machine that has about 2 pounds of the bread pan.

Add all the ingredients in the order revealed in the ingredients list into the bread machine pan.

Press the "Dough" button, press the start button, and let mixture knead for 5 to 10 minutes until all the ingredients have thoroughly combined and incorporated.

Select the "basic/white" cycle, key the up/down arrow to set baking time to 4 hours.

Select light or medium color for the crust, and press the start button.

Then sensibly lift out the bread, and put it on a wire rack for 1 hour or more until cooled. Cut bread into twelve slices and then serve.

CRANBERRY WALNUT BREAD

Grain, Seed and Nut Bread

10 minutes *4 hours* *16 servings*

INGREDIENTS

1 1/3 Milk, lukewarm

2 tbsp Butter, unsalted, softened

3 tablespoons honey

2/3 cups of bread flour

1 teaspoon salt

1 teaspoon active dry yeast

1 cup Dried cranberries

1 cup Walnuts

HOW TO MAKE IT

Gather all the ingredients needed for the bread. Power on bread machine that has about 2 pounds of the bread pan.

Add all the ingredients except for nuts and cranberries into the bread machine pan in the order mentioned in the ingredients list.

Press the "Dough" button, press the start button, let mixture knead for 5 minutes, then add walnuts and cranberries and continue kneading for 5 minutes until all the ingredients have thoroughly combined and incorporated.

Select the "basic/white" cycle, press the up/down arrow to set baking time to 4 hours.

Select light or medium color for the crust, and press the start button. Then carefully lift the bread, and transfer it to a wire rack for 1 hour or additional until cooled. Cut bread into slices and then serve.

NUTRITION

Kcal: 123
Protein: 4 g
Fat: 2 g
Carbs: 24 g

PUMPKIN BREAD WITH WALNUTS

Grain, Seed and Nut Bread

10 minutes   *1 hour*   *16 sevings*

INGREDIENTS

¾ cup milk, lukewarm

3 tablespoons butter, melted at room temperature

1 tablespoon honey

¾ teaspoon ground nutmeg

½ teaspoon salt

1 ½ cups Pumpkin puree

3 cups white bread flour

2 ¼ teaspoons bread machine or active dry yeast

1 tsp Ground cinnamon

1 cup Chopped walnuts

HOW TO MAKE IT

Place all the ingredients needed for the bread. Power on bread machine that has about 2 pounds of the bread pan.

Take a large mixing bowl, add eggs to it and then beat in sugar, oil, and pumpkin puree using an electric mixer until smooth and well blended.

Beat in salt, all the spices, baking powder, and soda, and then beat in flour, ½-cup at a time, until incorporated. Pour the batter into the bread pan, top with nuts, select the "cake/quick bread" cycle, or press the up/down arrow to set baking time to 1 hour.

Choose light or medium color for the crust, and then press the start button. Then carefully get out the bread and hand it to a wire rack for 1 hour or more until cooled. Cut bread into sixteen slices and then serve.

NUTRITION

Kcal: 166
Protein: 3 g
Fat: 9 g
Carbs: 19 g

FLAX AND SUNFLOWER SEED BREAD

Fruit and Vegetable Bread

5 minutes   25 minutes   8 servings

INGREDIENTS

HOW TO MAKE IT

1 1/3 cups water

Two tablespoons butter softened

Three tablespoons honey

2/3 cups of bread flour

One teaspoon salt

One teaspoon active dry yeast

1/2 cup flax seeds

1/2 cup sunflower seeds

With the manufacturer's suggested order, add all the ingredients (apart from sunflower seeds) to the bread machine's pan.

The select basic white cycles, then press start.

Just in the knead cycle that your machine signals alert sounds, add the sunflower seeds.

NUTRITION

Kcal: 140
Protein: 4 g
Fat: 4 g
Carbs: 22 g

HONEY AND FLAXSEED BREAD

Grain, Seed and Nut Bread

5 minutes   25 minutes   8 sevings

INGREDIENTS

1 1/8 cups water

1 1/2 tablespoons flaxseed oil

Three tablespoons honey

1/2 tablespoon liquid lecithin

3 cups whole wheat flour

1/2 cup flax seed

2 tablespoons bread flour

3 tablespoons whey powder

1 1/2 teaspoons sea salt

2 teaspoons active dry yeast

HOW TO MAKE IT

In the bread machine pan, put in all of the ingredients following the order recommended by the manufacturer.

Choose the Wheat cycle on the machine and press the Start button to run the machine.

Take out the bread from the machine and let it cool down completely.

Slice the bread and serve.

NUTRITION

Kcal: 174
Protein: 7.1 g
Fat: 4.9 g
Carbs: 30.8 g

WALNUT BREAD

Grain, Seed and Nut Bread

20 minutes   *4 hours*   *10 sevings*

INGREDIENTS

4 cups almond flour

½ cup water

½ cup milk

2 eggs

½ cup walnuts

1 tablespoon vegetable oil

1 tablespoon sugar

1 teaspoon salt

1 teaspoon yeast

NUTRITION

Kcal: 169
Protein: 6 g
Fat: 1 g
Carbs: 32 g

HOW TO MAKE IT

Tip: All products must be room temperature.

Pour water, milk, and vegetable oil into the bucket and add in the eggs. Now pour in the sifted almond flour. In the process of kneading bread, you may need a little more or less flour – it depends on its moisture.

Pour in salt, sugar, and yeast. If it is hot in the kitchen (especially in summer), pour all three ingredients into the different ends of the bucket so that the dough does not have time for peroxide.

Now the first kneading dough begins, which lasts 15 minutes. In the process, we monitor the state of the ball. It should be soft, but at the same time, keep its shape and not spread. If the ball does not want to be collected, add a little flour, since the moisture of this product is different for everyone. If the bucket is clean and all the flour is incorporated into the dough, then everything is done right. If the dough is still lumpy and even crumbles, you need to add a little more liquid.

Close the lid and then prepare the nuts. They need to be sorted and lightly fried in a dry frying pan; the pieces of nuts will be crispy. Then let them cool and cut with a knife to the desired size. When the bread maker signals, pour in the nuts and wait until the spatula mixes them into the dough. Remove the bucket and take out the walnut bread. Completely cool it on a grill so that the bottom does not get wet.

Bon Appetite, friends!

APPLE & PISTACHIOS BREAD

Grain, Seed and Nut Bread

20 minutes   *3h 30min*   *8 sevings*

NUTRITION

Kcal: 291
Protein: 7.7 g
Fat: 10.9 g
Carbs: 2 g

INGREDIENTS

3 cups almond flour

2 eggs

3 tbsp. grated horseradish

½ cup apple puree

1 tbsp. sugar

4 tbsp. olive oil

½ cup peeled pistachios

1 tsp. dried yeast

1 tsp. salt

HOW TO MAKE IT

Lightly beat eggs in a bowl. Pour in enough water to make 280 ml of liquid. Pour into a mold, and add olive oil.

Put in the flour, applesauce, horseradish, and half the pistachios. Add salt and sugar from different angles. Make a small groove in the flour and put in the yeast.

Bake on the BASIC program. After the final mixing of the dough, moisten the surface of the product with water and sprinkle with the remaining pistachios.
When finished, carefully remove the loaf and let it cool down.

BRUCE'S HONEY SESAME BREAD

1 1/4 cups water

1 tbsp. powdered buttermilk

3 cups bread flour

Three tbsp. wheat bran

1/2 cup sesame seeds, toasted

2 1/4 tsp. active dry yeast

1/4 cup honey 1

1/2 tsp. salt

Into the bread machine's pan, place all the ingredients by following the order endorsed by your machine's manufacturer.

Set the mechanism to the BASIC Bread cycle.

When finished, remove the loaf and let it cool down before slicing and serving.

NUTRITION Kcal: 820, Protein: 22 g, Fat: 16 g, Carbs: 145 g

MULTI-GRAIN BREAD

Grain, Seed and Nut Bread

20 minutes   *6 hours*   *10 sevings*

INGREDIENTS

sugar to taste

1 teaspoon salt

1 ½ tablespoon olive oil

1 ½ teaspoons dry yeast

1 ½ tablespoons flower honey

1 ½ tablespoons pumpkin seeds

½ cup milk

1 ½ cups almond flour

½ cup barley flour

½ cup whole wheat flour

1 ½ tablespoon sunflower seeds

milk to taste

salt to taste

NUTRITION

Kcal: 169
Protein: 6 g
Fat: 1 g
Carbs: 32 g

HOW TO MAKE IT

In a small bowl crush the yeast. Rub their hands with 2 tablespoons of wheat flour.

Add a pinch of sugar and ½ cup of salted water at room temperature. Cover with a towel and leave for 10 minutes.

In the bowl of the bread maker, mix all the remaining flour (pre-sift it), seeds, and nuts. Add the yeast, ¼ cup of warm water, and milk at room temperature. Start mixing the dough. It should be slightly sticky.

Add olive oil and honey. Continue to knead. When the dough becomes soft, collect it in one lump, coat with olive oil, and transfer to a large bowl.

Cover it with food film and transfer it to the refrigerator for fermentation for 12 hours.

Remove the dough from the fridge. After an hour, let it rest at room temperature. Transfer to the bowl of the bread maker for 1 hour.

Lubricate the loaf with milk and sprinkle with salt. Proceed with the bread maker's baking cycle as directed. Take the finished bread from the bowl, put it on a grate, and let it cool completely.

CHIA SEED BREAD

Grain, Seed and Nut Bread

20 minutes *3h 10 min* *16 sevings*

INGREDIENTS

4 Tbsp. chia seeds

1/3 cup flax meal

2 cups almond flour

1½ cup coconut flour

1 tsp. sea salt

1 tsp. baking soda

2 tsp. bread machine yeast

¼ cup coconut oil, melted

NUTRITION

Kcal: 337
Protein: 11.8g
Fat: 17.7g
Carbs: 32.8g

HOW TO MAKE IT

In a small bowl, combine the chia seeds and 1 teaspoon of flax meal with water and let it rest until it becomes a gel.

In a medium-sized bowl, whisk together coconut oil, maple syrup, eggs, and almond milk. The maple syrup is necessary for activating the yeast, and it will be completely absorbed. It will not impact the total carb count.

Add the chia seed/flax meal gel to the medium-sized bowl and continue whisking.

Pour the wet mixture into the bread machine pan and put the remaining ingredients (except yeast) on the top.

Place the yeast in the center of the bread mix. Close the cover. Set your bread machine program to WHOLE GRAIN and choose the crust color MEDIUM. Press START.

Wait until the program is complete. When done, take the bucket out and let it cool for 5-10 minutes.

Shake the loaf from the pan and let cool for 30 minutes on a cooling rack. Slice, serve, and enjoy the taste of fragrant homemade keto bread.

SEED AND NUT BREAD

Grain, Seed and Nut Bread

20 minutes   *40 minutes*   *24 sevings*

INGREDIENTS

3 eggs

¼ cup avocado oil

5 tsp. psyllium husk powder

1 tsp. apple cider vinegar

¾ tsp. salt

5 drops liquid stevia

1 ½ cups raw unsalted almonds

½ cup raw unsalted pepitas

½ cup raw unsalted sunflower

seeds

½ cup flaxseeds

NUTRITION

Kcal: 131
Protein: 11.8g
Fat: 5 g
Carbs: 4 g

HOW TO MAKE IT

Prepare bread machine loaf pan greasing it with cooking spray.

In a large bowl, whisk together the oil, eggs, psyllium husk powder, vinegar, salt, and liquid stevia. Stir in the pepitas, almonds, sunflower seeds, and flaxseeds until well combined. However, take a look to the manufacturer's instructions for mixing dry and wet ingredients.

Pour mixture in the bread machine loaf pan. Place the bread pan in the machine, and select the basic bread setting, together with the bread size, if available, then press start once you have closed the lid of the machine.

When the bread is ready, using oven mitts, remove the bread pan from the machine. Cool, slice, and serve.

BAGELS WITH POPPY SEEDS

Grain, Seed and Nut Bread

 5 minutes

 25 minutes

 8 sevings

INGREDIENTS

1 cup of warm water

1 1/2 teaspoons salt

Two tablespoons white sugar

3 cups bread flour

2 1/4 teaspoons active dry yeast

3 quarts boiling water

Three tablespoons white sugar

One tablespoon cornmeal

One egg white

Three tablespoons poppy seeds

NUTRITION

Kcal: 337
Protein: 11.8g
Fat: 17.7g
Carbs: 32.8g

HOW TO MAKE IT

In the bread machine's pan, pour in the water, salt, sugar, flour, and yeast following the order of ingredients suggested by the manufacturer. Choose the DOUGH setting on the machine.

Once the machine has finished the whole cycle, place the dough on a clean surface covered with a little bit of flour; let it rest. While the dough is resting on the floured surface, put 3 quarts of water in a big pot and let it boil.
Add in 3 tablespoons of sugar and mix.

Divide the dough evenly into nine portions and shape each into a small ball. Press down each dough ball until it is flat. Use your thumb to make a shack in the center of each flattened dough. Increase the hole's size in the center and smoothen out the dough around the hole area by spinning the dough on your thumb or finger.

Use a clean cloth to cover the formed bagels and let it sit for 10 minutes. Cover the bottom part of an ungreased baking sheet evenly with cornmeal. Place the bagels gently into the boiling water. Let it boil for 1 minute and flip it on the other side halfway through. Let the bagels drain quickly on a clean towel. Place the boiled bagels onto the prepared baking sheet.

Coat the topmost of each bagel with egg white and top it off with your preferred toppings.
Put the bagels into the preheated 375°F (190°C) oven and bake for 20-25 minutes until it turns nice brown.

PARMESAN TOMATO BASIL BREAD

Cheese Bread

5 minutes   2 hours   10 servings

INGREDIENTS

¼ cup Sun-dried tomatoes,

chopped

2 tsp. Yeast

2 cups bread flour

1/3 cup parmesan cheese, grated

2 tsp. dried basil

1 tsp sugar

2 tbsp olive oil

¼ cup milk

½ cup water

1 tsp salt

HOW TO MAKE IT

Add all ingredients except for sun-dried tomatoes into the bread machine pan. Select the basic setting, then select medium crust and press start.

Add sun-dried tomatoes just before the final kneading cycle.

Take the pan of bread out of the oven after it's finished baking. Ten minutes is all it takes for it to cool.

Cut into individual servings.

NUTRITION

Kcal: 183
Protein: 7.9 g
Fat: 6.8 g
Carbs: 20.3 g

CHEESE BUTTERMILK BREAD

Cheese Bread

5 minutes   2 hour   10 sevings

NUTRITION

Kcal: 182
Protein: 7 g
Fat: 3.5 g
Carbs: 30.6 g

INGREDIENTS

1 1/8 cups Buttermilk

1 ½ tsp. Active dry yeast

¾ cup. shredded Cheddar cheese

1 ½ tsp. Sugar

3 cups Bread flour

1 1/8 cups Buttermilk

1 1/2 tsp. Salt

HOW TO MAKE IT

Place all ingredients into the bread machine pan based on the bread machine manufacturer instructions.

Select **BASIC** bread setting, then select light/medium crust and START.

After the bread is finished baking, take it out of the oven. Ten minutes will do it. Slice and enjoy!

BEER CHEESE BREAD

4 oz Monterey J. cheese shredded

4 oz. American cheese shredded

10 oz. beer

1 tbsp. butter + 1 tbsp. sugar

3 cups bread flour

1 packet Active dry yeast

1 ½ tsp. Salt

Place the ingredients into the pan of the bread machine. Select the BASIC setting, and then select a light crust and START.

Once the loaf is done, remove the loaf pan from the machine. Allow it to cool for 10 minutes. Slice and serve.

NUTRITION Kcal: 820, Protein: 22 g, Fat: 16 g, Carbs: 145 g

DELICIOUS ITALIAN CHEESE BREAD

Cheese Bread

5 minutes	25 minutes	8 servings

INGREDIENTS

1 1/3 cups water

Two tablespoons butter softened

Three tablespoons honey

2/3 cups of bread flour

One teaspoon salt

One teaspoon active dry yeast

1/2 cup flax seeds

1/2 cup sunflower seeds

HOW TO MAKE IT

With the manufacturer's suggested order, add all the ingredients (apart from sunflower seeds) to the bread machine's pan.

The select basic white cycles, then press start.

Just in the knead cycle that your machine signals alert sounds, add the sunflower seeds.

NUTRITION

Kcal: 163
Protein: 5 g
Fat: 2 g
Carbs: 31 g

MOIST CHEDDAR CHEESE BREAD

Cheese Bread

---

5 minutes *3h 45 min* *10 sevings*

INGREDIENTS

1 cup Milk

½ cup Butter, melted

3 cups All-purpose flour

2 cups Cheddar cheese, shredded

½ tsp. Garlic powder

2 tsp. Kosher salt

1 tbsp. Sugar

1 ¼ oz. Active dry yeast

NUTRITION

Kcal: 337
Protein: 11.8g
Fat: 17.7g
Carbs: 32.8g

HOW TO MAKE IT

Add milk and butter into the bread pan. Add remaining ingredients except for yeast to the bread pan.

Make a narrow hole into the flour with your finger and add yeast to the punch.

Make sure yeast will not be mixed with any liquids.

Select the basic setting, and then select a light crust and start. Once the loaf is done, remove the loaf pan from the machine.

Allow it to cool for 10 minutes. Slice and serve.

CHEESE PEPPERONI BREAD

Cheese Bread

5 minutes   *2 hours*   *10 servings*

INGREDIENTS

2/3 cup Pepperoni, diced

1 ½ tsp. Active dry yeast

3 ¼ cups. Bread flour

1 ½ tsp. Dried oregano

1 ½ tsp. Garlic salt

2 tbsp. Sugar

1/3 cup. Mozzarella cheese

1 cup+2 tbsp. Warm water

HOW TO MAKE IT

Add all ingredients except for pepperoni into the bread machine pan. Select basic setting, then selects medium crust and press start.

Add pepperoni just before the final kneading cycle.

The pan should be removed from the machine after the bread has finished baking.

Let it rest for ten minutes. Slice into pieces and present.

NUTRITION

Kcal: 176
Protein: 5.7 g
Fat: 1.5g
Carbs: 34.5g

GARLIC PARMESAN BREAD

Cheese Bread

5 minutes   3h 45 min   10 sevings

INGREDIENTS

¼ oz. Active dry yeast

3 tbsp. Sugar

2 tsp. Kosher salt

1 tsp. Dried oregano

1 tsp. Dried basil

½ tsp. Garlic powder

½ cup Parmesan cheese, grated

3 ½ cups All-purpose flour

1 tbsp. Garlic, minced

¼ cup Butter, melted

1/3 cup Olive oil

1 1/3 cups Water

HOW TO MAKE IT

Add water, oil, butter, and garlic into the bread pan. Add remaining ingredients except for yeast to the bread pan.

Make a small hole in the flour with your finger and add yeast to the spot.

Make sure yeast will not be mixed with any liquids.

Select the basic setting, then selects a light crust and start. Once the loaf is done, remove the loaf pan from the machine.

Allow it to cool for 10 minutes. Slice and serve.

NUTRITION

Kcal: 335
Protein: 9.7g
Fat: 15.4g
Carbs: 37.7g

CHEESE JALAPENO BREAD

Cheese Bread

5 minutes   *2 hours*   *10 servings*

INGREDIENTS

1 1/3 cups water

Two tablespoons butter softened

Three tablespoons honey

2/3 cups of bread flour

One teaspoon salt

One teaspoon active dry yeast

1/2 cup flax seeds

1/2 cup sunflower seeds

½ cup gruyere cheese, grated

2/3 cup jalapeno, sliced

HOW TO MAKE IT

Begin by adding all fixings to the bread machine pan according to the bread machine manufacturer instructions.

Select basic bread setting, and then select light/medium crust and start.

Once the loaf is done, remove the loaf pan from the machine.

Allow it to cool for 10 minutes. Slice and serve.

NUTRITION

Kcal: 174
Protein: 5.1g
Fat: 3.1g
Carbs: 31.1g

93
ITALIAN HERB CHEESE BREAD

Cheese Bread

---

5 minutes	*3 hours*	*10 sevings*

INGREDIENTS

1 ½ tsp. Yeast

1 tbsp. Italian herb seasoning

2 tbsp. Brown sugar

1 cup. Cheddar cheese, shredded

3 cups. Bread flour

4 tbsp. Butter

1 ¼ cups. Warm milk

2 tsp. Salt

NUTRITION

Kcal: 247
Protein: 8.7g
Fat: 9.4g
Carbs: 32.7g

HOW TO MAKE IT

Add milk into the bread pan, then add remaining ingredients except for yeast to the bread pan.

Make a small hole into the flour with your finger and add yeast to the spot. Make sure yeast will not be mixed with any liquids.

Select a basic setting, then selects a light crust and start.

Once the loaf is done, remove the loaf pan from the machine.

Allow it to cool for 10 minutes. Slice and serve.

CHEDDAR CHEESE BASIL BREAD

Cheese Bread

5 minutes   *3 hours*   *10 servings*

INGREDIENTS

1 ½ tsp. Yeast

1 tbsp. Italian herb seasoning

2 tbsp. Brown sugar

1 cup. Cheddar cheese, shredded

3 cups. Bread flour

4 tbsp. Butter

1 ¼ cups. Warm milk

2 tsp. Salt

NUTRITION

Kcal: 174
Protein: 5.1g
Fat: 3.1g
Carbs: 31.1g

HOW TO MAKE IT

Preparing the Ingredients. Place the ingredients in your Zojirushi bread machine.

Select either light or medium crust, program the machine to Regular Basic, and hit Start.

After the bread has finished baking, take the bucket out of the oven. Wait five minutes for the bread to cool.

Softly shake the canister to remove the loaf and put it out onto a rack to cool.

95

CINNAMON & DRIED FRUITS BREAD

Spice & Herbs Bread

5 minutes   *3 hours*   *16 slices*

INGREDIENTS

2¾ cups flour

1½ cups dried fruits

4 tablespoons sugar

2½ tablespoons butter

1 tablespoon milk powder

1 teaspoon cinnamon

½ teaspoon ground nutmeg

¼ teaspoon vanillin

½ cup peanuts

powdered sugar, for sprinkling

1 teaspoon salt

1½ bread machine yeast

HOW TO MAKE IT

Add all of the ingredients to your bread machine (except peanuts and powdered sugar), carefully following the instructions of the manufacturer.

Set the program of your bread machine to Basic/White Bread and set crust type to Medium.

Once the bread maker beeps, moisten dough with a bit of water and add peanuts.

Wait until the cycle completes. Once the loaf is ready, take the bucket out and let the loaf cool for 5 minutes.

Gently shake the bucket to remove the loaf. Sprinkle with powdered sugar.

NUTRITION

Kcal: 73
Protein: 3 g
Fat: 4 g
Carbs: 8 g

LOVELY AROMATIC LAVENDER BREAD

Spice & Herbs Bread

---

5 minutes

2 h 45min

8 sevings

INGREDIENTS

HOW TO MAKE IT

¾ cup milk at 80 degrees F

1 tablespoon melted butter, cooled

1 tablespoon sugar

¾ teaspoon salt

1 teaspoon fresh lavender flower, chopped

¼ teaspoon lemon zest

¼ teaspoon fresh thyme, chopped

2 cups white bread flour

¾ teaspoon instant yeast

Add all of the ingredients to your bread maker and carefully follow the manufacturer's directions.

Set your bread machine's program to Basic/White Bread and the crust type to Medium. Wait till the cycle is finished.

When the loaf is done, remove it from the bucket and set it aside for 5 minutes to cool.

Gently shake the bucket to remove the loaf.

NUTRITION

Kcal: 156
Protein: 5 g
Fat: 8 g
Carbs: 17 g

HERBAL GARLIC CREAM CHEESE DELIGHT

Spice & Herbs Bread

5 minutes   *2 h 45min*   *8 sevings*

INGREDIENTS

1/3 cup water at 80 degrees F

1/3 cup herb and garlic cream cheese mix, at room temp

1 whole egg, beaten, at room temp

4 teaspoons melted butter, cooled

1 tablespoon sugar

2/3 teaspoon salt

2 cups white bread flour

1 teaspoon instant yeast

NUTRITION

Kcal: 73
Protein: 3 g
Fat: 4 g
Carbs: 8 g

HOW TO MAKE IT

Add all of the ingredients to your bread machine, carefully following the instructions of the manufacturer.

Set the program of your bread machine to Basic/White Bread and set crust type to Medium.

Wait until the cycle completes.

Once the loaf is ready, take the bucket out and let the loaf cool for 5 minutes.

Gently shake the bucket to remove the loaf. Slice & serve.

OREGANO
MOZZA-CHEESE BREAD

Spice & Herbs Bread

15 minutes   *3h 45min*   *16 sevings*

INGREDIENTS

HOW TO MAKE IT

1 cup (milk + egg) mixture

½ cup mozzarella cheese

2¼ cups flour

¾ cup whole grain flour

2 tablespoons sugar

1 teaspoon salt

2 teaspoons oregano

1½ teaspoons dry yeast

Add all of the ingredients to your bread machine, carefully following the instructions of the manufacturer.

Set the program of your bread machine to Basic/White Bread and set crust type to Dark.

Wait until the cycle completes.

Once the loaf is ready, take the bucket out and let the loaf cool for 5 minutes.

Gently shake the bucket to remove the loaf.

NUTRITION

Kcal: 156
Protein: 5 g
Fat: 8 g
Carbs: 17 g

99

CUMIN TOSSED FANCY BREAD

Spice & Herbs Bread

5 minutes   *3h 15min*   *16 sevings*

NUTRITION

Kcal: 368
Protein: 9 g
Fat: 7.5 g
Carbs: 67.6 g

INGREDIENTS

HOW TO MAKE IT

5 1/3 cups wheat flour

3 tablespoons sunflower oil

1½ teaspoons salt

1½ tablespoons sugar

1 tablespoon dry yeast

1¾ cups water

2 tablespoons cumin

Add warm water to the bread machine bucket. Then add salt, sugar, and sunflower oil. Sift in wheat flour and add yeast.

Set the program of your bread machine to French bread and set crust type to Medium. Once the maker beeps, add cumin and wait until the cycle completes.

Once the loaf is ready, take the bucket out and let the loaf cool for 5 minutes. Gently shake the bucket to remove the loaf.

100 POTATO ROSEMARY LOAF

4 cups wheat flour

1 tablespoon sugar

1½ teaspoons salt

1½ cups water

1 teaspoon dry yeast

1 tablespoon sunflower oil

1 cup mashed potatoes

crushed rosemary to taste

Add flour, salt, and sugar to the bread maker bucket and attach mixing paddle. Then add sunflower oil and water and put in yeast as directed.

Set the program of your bread machine to Bread with Filling mode and set crust type to Medium.

Once the bread maker beeps and signals to add more ingredients, open lid, add mashed potatoes, and chopped rosemary. Wait until the cycle completes.

Once the loaf is ready, take the bucket out and let the loaf cool for 5 minutes. Gently shake the bucket to remove the loaf.

CAJUN BREAD

Spice & Herbs Bread

10 minutes	*2h 10min*	*14 sevings*

INGREDIENTS

½ cup water

¼ cup chopped onion

¼ cup chopped green bell pepper

2 teaspoon finely chopped garlic

2 teaspoon soft butter

2 cups bread flour

1 Tablespoon sugar

1 teaspoon Cajun

½ teaspoon salt

1 teaspoon active dry yeast

NUTRITION

Kcal: 150
Protein: 5 g
Fat: 4 g
Carbs: 23 g

HOW TO MAKE IT

Add each ingredient to the bread machine in the order and at the temperature recommended by your bread machine manufacturer.

Close the lid; select the basic bread, medium crust setting on your bread machine and press start.

When the bread machine has finished baking, remove the bread and put it on a cooling rack.

102

INSPIRING CINNAMON BREAD

Spice & Herbs Bread

15 minutes   *2 h 15min*   *8 sevings*

INGREDIENTS

2/3 cup milk at 80 degrees F

1 whole egg, beaten

3 tablespoons melted butter, cooled

1/3 cup sugar

1/3 teaspoon salt

1 teaspoon ground cinnamon

2 cups white bread flour

1 1/3 teaspoons active dry yeast

NUTRITION

Kcal: 198
Protein: 5 g
Fat: 5 g
Carbs: 34 g

HOW TO MAKE IT

Add all of the ingredients to your bread machine, carefully following the instructions of the manufacturer.

Set the program of your bread machine to Basic/White Bread and set crust type to Medium.

Wait until the cycle completes.

Once the loaf is ready, take the bucket out and let the loaf cool for 5 minutes. Remove the loaf

HONEY LAVANDER BREAD

Spice & Herbs Bread

10 minutes   *3h 25min*   *16 sevings*

INGREDIENTS

1½ cups wheat flour

2 1/3 cups whole meal flour

1 teaspoon fresh yeast

1½ cups water

1 teaspoon lavender

1½ tablespoons honey

1 teaspoon salt

HOW TO MAKE IT

Sift both types of flour into a mixing dish and combine. Add all of the ingredients to your bread maker and carefully follow the manufacturer's directions.

Set the program of your bread machine to Basic/White Bread and set crust type to Medium. Wait until the cycle completes.

Once the loaf is ready, take the bucket out and let the loaf cool for 5 minutes. Gently shake the bucket to remove the loaf.

TURMERIC BREAD

1 teaspoon dried yeast

4 cups strong white flour

1 teaspoon turmeric powder

2 teaspoon beetroot powder

2 Tablespoon olive oil

1.5 teaspoon salt

1 teaspoon chili flakes

1 3/8 water

Add each ingredient to the bread machine in the order and at the temperature recommended by your bread machine manufacturer.

Close the lid; select the basic bread, medium crust setting on your bread machine and press start.

When the bread machine has finished baking, remove the bread and put it on a cooling rack.

NUTRITION he starter has to be fed, active, and at room

105

HAZELNUT HONEY BREAD

Sweet Bread

5 minutes *45 minutes* *10 slices*

INGREDIENTS

½ cup lukewarm milk

2 teaspoons liquid honey

2 teaspoons butter, melted and cooled

1/3 cup cooked wild rice, cooled

1/3 cup whole grain flour

1 cup almond flour, sifted

/3 teaspoons caraway seeds

2/3 teaspoons salt

1/3 cup hazelnuts, chopped

1 teaspoon active dry yeast

HOW TO MAKE IT

Prepare all of the Ingredients for your bread and measuring means (a cup, a spoon, kitchen scales).

Carefully measure the Ingredients into the pan, except the nuts and seeds. Place all of the Ingredients, into the bread bucket in the right order, following the manual for your bread machine. Close the cover.

Select the program of your bread machine to basic and choose the crust color to medium. Press start.

After the signal, add the nuts and seeds into the dough. Wait until the program completes. When done, take the bucket out and let it cool for 5-10 minutes.

Shake the loaf from the pan and let cool for 30 minutes on a cooling rack. Slice, serve, and enjoy the taste of fragrant homemade bread.

NUTRITION

Kcal: 73
Protein: 3 g
Fat: 4 g
Carbs: 8 g

SWEET ROSEMARY BREAD

Sweet Bread

NUTRITION

Kcal: 156
Protein: 5 g
Fat: 8 g
Carbs: 17 g

5 minutes   *15min*   *12 sevings*

INGREDIENTS

2 ½ cups almond flour

¼ cup coconut flour

½ cup ghee

8 oz. cream cheese

5 eggs

1 tsp rosemary

1 tsp sage, ground

2 tsp parsley

1 tsp baking powder

HOW TO MAKE IT

Slightly beat eggs and ghee together in a bowl then pour into bread machine pan. Add all the remaining ingredients.

Set bread machine to the French bread setting. When the bread is done, remove bread machine pan from the bread machine.

Let cool slightly before transferring to a cooling rack.
You can store your bread for up to 7 days in the refrigerator.

COCONUT FLOUR BREAD

 6 eggs

 ½ cup coconut flour

 2 tbsp. psyllium husk

 ¼ cup olive oil

 1 ½ tsp salt

 1 tsp. xanthan gum

 2 ¼ tsp yeast

 1 tsp. baking powder

Use a small mixing bowl to combine all dry ingredients, except for the yeast. In the bread machine pan add all wet ingredients.

Add all of your dry ingredients, from the small mixing bowl, in the bread machine pan. Top with the yeast.

Set the bread machine to the basic bread setting. When the bread is done, remove bread machine pan from the bread machine. Let cool slightly before transferring to a cooling rack.

The bread can be stored for up to 4 days on the counter and for up to 3 months in the freezer.

CINNAMON ALMOND BREAD

Sweet Bread

3 minutes *15 minutes* *10 sevings*

INGREDIENTS

2 tbsps. Coconut flour

1 tsp baking soda

2 cups almond flour

2 tbsps. Coconut oil

¼ cup flaxseed, ground

1 egg white

1 ½ tsp lemon juice

5 eggs

2 tbsps. Erythritol

½ tsp salt

1 tbsp. cinnamon

NUTRITION

Kcal: 220
Protein: 9 g
Fat: 15 g
Carbs: 10 g

HOW TO MAKE IT

Pour wet ingredients into bread machine pan. Now add the dry ingredients to the machine pan.

Set bread machine to the gluten free setting.

When the bread is done, remove bread machine pan from the bread machine.

Let cool slightly before transferring to a cooling rack. You can store your bread for up to 5 days.

ALMOND FLOUR BREAD

Sweet Bread

4 minutes   *15 minutes*   *10 sevings*

INGREDIENTS

4 egg whites

2 egg yolks

2 cups almond flour

¼ cup butter, melted

2 tbsp. psyllium husk powder

1 ½ tsp baking powder

½ tsp xanthan gum

Salt

½ cup + 2 tbsps. Warm water

2 ¼ tsp yeast

HOW TO MAKE IT

Use a small mixing bowl to combine all dry ingredients, except for the yeast.

In the bread machine pan add all wet ingredients. Add all of your dry ingredients, from the small mixing bowl, in the bread machine pan. Top with the yeast.

Set the bread machine to the basic bread setting. When the bread is done, remove bread machine pan from the bread machine.

Let cool slightly before transferring to a cooling rack. The bread can be stored for up to 4 days on the counter and for up to 3 months in the freezer.

NUTRITION

Kcal: 110
Protein: 4 g
Fat: 10 g
Carbs: 2.3 g

BANANA CAKE LOAF

Sweet Bread

5 minutes

15 minutes

12 sevings

NUTRITION

Kcal: 182
Protein: 7 g
Fat: 3.5 g
Carbs: 30.6 g

INGREDIENTS

1 ½ cups almond flour

1 tsp baking powder

½ cup butter

1 ½ cups erythritol

2 eggs

2 bananas, extra ripe, mashed

2 tsp whole milk

HOW TO MAKE IT

Mix butter, eggs, and milk together in a mixing bowl. Mash bananas with a fork and add in the mashed bananas.

Mix all dry ingredients together in a separate small bowl. Slowly combine dry ingredients with wet ingredients.

Pour mixture into bread machine pan. Set bread machine for bake. When the cake is done remove from bread machine and transfer to a cooling rack.

Allow to cool completely before serving. You can store your banana cake loaf bread for up to 5 days in the refrigerator.

111   CINNAMON CAKE

INGREDIENTS

½ cup erythritol

½ cup butter

½ tbsp. vanilla extract

1 ¾ cups almond flour

1 ½ tsp baking powder

1 ½ tsp cinnamon

¼ tsp sea salt

1 ½ cup carrots, grated

1 cup pecans, chopped

HOW TO MAKE IT

Grate carrots and place in a food processor. Add in the rest of the ingredients, except the pecans, and process until well-incorporated. Fold in pecans.
Pour mixture into bread machine pan and set bread machine to bake.

When baking is complete remove from bread machine and transfer to a cooling rack. Allow to cool completely before slicing. (You can also top with a sugar-free cream cheese frosting, see recipe below).

You can store for up to 5 days in the refrigerator.

NOT YOUR EVERYDAY BREAD

Sweet Bread

10 minutes	2h 10min	14 sevings

INGREDIENTS

2 tsp active dry yeast

2 tbsp. inulin

½ cup warm water

¾ cup almond flour

¼ cup golden flaxseed, ground

2 tbsp. whey Protein isolate

2 tbsp. psyllium husk finely ground

2 tsp xanthan gum

2 tsp baking powder

1 tsp salt

¼ tsp cream of tartar

¼ tsp ginger, ground

1 egg

3 egg whites

2 tbsp. ghee

1 tbsp. apple cider vinegar

¼ cup sour cream

HOW TO MAKE IT

Pour wet ingredients into bread machine pan. Add dry ingredients, with the yeast on top.

Set bread machine to basic bread setting.

When the bread is done, remove bread machine pan from the bread machine.

Let cool slightly before transferring to a cooling rack.

You can store your bread for up to 5 days.

NUTRITION

Kcal: 150
Protein: 5 g
Fat: 4 g
Carbs: 23 g

RASPBERRY BREAD

Sweet Bread

 15 minutes   *15 minutes*   *9 sevings*

NUTRITION

Kcal: 156
Protein: 5 g
Fat: 8 g
Carbs: 17 g

INGREDIENTS

2 cups almond flour

½ cup coconut flour

½ cup ghee

½ cup coconut oil, melted

½ cup erythritol

4 eggs

1 tsp lemon juice

½ cup raspberries

2 tsp baking powder

HOW TO MAKE IT

Lightly beat eggs before pouring into bread machine pan. Add in melted coconut oil, ghee, and lemon juice to pan. Add the remaining ingredients.

Set bread machine to quick bread. When the bread is done, remove bread machine pan from the bread machine.

Let cool slightly before transferring to a cooling rack.

You can store your bread for up to 5 days.

WHOLE-WHEAT SOURDOUGH BREAD

2/3 cups hot water

2/3 cup No-Yeast

Whole-Wheat Sourdough Starter,

4 teaspoons butter, melted

1¼ teaspoons instant yeast

2 cups whole- almond flour

2 teaspoons sugar

1 teaspoon salt

Put all ingredients in the bread machine and set the machine to Whole-Wheat/Whole-Grain bread, select light or medium crust, press Start.

When ready, remove the bread and allow about 5 minutes cooling the loaf. Put it on a rack to cool it completely.

tip: The starter has to be fed, active, and at room temperature

ORANGE ROLLS

Sweet Bread

25 minutes   *3h 10min*   *20 rolls*

INGREDIENTS

For the dough:

¼ cup heavy cream, warmed

½ cup orange juice concentrate

2 Tbsp. sugar

1 tsp salt

1 large egg + 1 yolk

6 Tbsp. unsalted butter, softened

3 cups all-purpose flour

2 tsp bread machine yeast

For the filling:

2 Tbsp. unsalted butter, softened

½ cup sugar + 2 Tbsp. grated orange zest mixture

For the icing:

¼ cup heavy cream

¼ cup sugar

2 Tbsp. orange juice concentrate

2 Tbsp. unsalted butter

1/8 tsp salt

HOW TO MAKE IT

Add each ingredient for the dough to bread machine following the manufacturer's order.

Select the DOUGH cycle and press start. When it is finished, the dough should have doubled in size.

Move the dough from the bread machine to a floured surface. Roll the dough into rectangle. Cover it with butter and the sugar-orange zest mixture.

Roll the dough tightly and slowly from the long side, then cut into quarters. Cut the quarters into 5 evenly-sized rolls. Put them onto greased pan, cover it with towel, and let them rise for 45 minutes in a warm place.

Bake at 325°F in a preheated oven for 25-30 minutes.

Add each of the icing Ingredients: to a saucepan. Mix and cook over a medium heat until the mixture is syrupy. Let it cool. Pour icing over warm rolls and serve.

NUTRITION

Kcal: 150
Protein: 5 g
Fat: 4 g
Carbs: 23 g

DELICATE CRUST ALMOND BREAD

Sweet Bread

20 minutes *3h 30min* *8 sevings*

NUTRITION

Kcal: 344
Protein: 8.9 g
Fat: 4.9 g
Carbs: 4.5 g

INGREDIENTS

1 ¼ cups milk

5 ¼ cups almond flour

2 tbsp. vegetable oil

2 tbsp. sour cream

2 tsp. dried yeast

1 tbsp. sugar

2 tsp. salt

HOW TO MAKE IT

Pour the milk into the form and ½ cup of water, and then add flour.

Put butter, sugar, and salt in different corners of the mold. Make a groove in the flour and add the yeast.

Bake on the BASIC program.

After the final mixing of the dough, smear the surface of the product with sour cream. Cool, serve, enjoy!

RICE BREAD

4 ½ cups almond flour

1 cup, rice, cooked

1 egg

2 tablespoons milk powder

2 teaspoons dried yeast

2 tablespoons butter

1 tablespoon sugar

2 teaspoons salt

Pour 1 ¼ cups of water into the mold; add the egg. Add flour, rice, and milk powder. Put butter, sugar, and salt in different corners of the mold. Make a groove in the flour, and put in the yeast.

Bake on the BASIC program.

When ready, carefully remove the loaf and let it cool down.

ENGLISH MUFFIN

Donuts, Holiday Bread

5 minutes   *10 minutes*   *2 muffins*

INGREDIENTS

HOW TO MAKE IT

1-1/4 cups warm water

3 Tbsp Honey

3 tsp active dry yeast

1/2 tsp salt

3 cups bread flour

3/4 cups whole wheat flour

2 Tbsp butter ,

softened or room temperature

tip:
Honey and sugar have
an even 1 to 1 swap ratio.

NUTRITION

Kcal: 73
Protein: 3 g
Fat: 4 g
Carbs: 8 g

Load the bread machine starting with the warm water, yeast and honey. Check that the yeast is bubbling and foaming. If not, the yeast has gone bad and the bread will not rise. This is a common bread mishap.

Next, add the dry ingredients and butter and set the machine to the 1.5lb loaf and use the dough or manual cycle depending on your manufacturer.

Once the cycle is fully completed, turn the dough out from the machine onto a lightly floured surface. If the dough is too sticky to work with, knead in a bit of extra bread flour. Shape the dough into a log about 12 inches long.

Then cut it into uniform 1-inch pieces (12 total). Shape each piece into a ball (or a circle) and then lightly press flat between palms or hands to form the muffin shape and size.

Place the muffins on a cookie sheet lightly coated with cornmeal (optional) or lightly sprayed with non-stick oil to keep them from sticking during the second rise.

Allow them to rise for about 1 hour or until they double in size. This can be as short as 40 minutes, but the full 60 minutes results in a much taller muffin with more nooks and crannies. Both rise times taste great but the latter yields a better look and texture.

Using an electric griddle set to 300 degrees F or a non-stick skillet over medium-high heat, cook the muffins for 4 minutes on each side or until golden brown.

119

ITALIAN EASTER CAKE

Donuts, Holiday Bread

 10 minutes   *3 hours*   *6 sevings*

NUTRITION

Kcal: 190
Protein: 4 g
Fat: 5.5 g
Carbs: 34.6 g

INGREDIENTS

1¾ cups wheat flour

2½ Tbsp. quick dry yeast

8 Tbsp. sugar

½ tsp salt

3 chicken eggs

¾ cup milk

3 Tbsp. butter

1 cup raisins

HOW TO MAKE IT

Add each ingredient except the raisins to the bread machine in the order and at the temperature recommended by your bread machine manufacturer.

Close the lid; select the SWEET loaf, LOW crust setting on your bread machine, and press start.

When the dough is kneading, add the raisins.

When the bread machine has finished baking, remove the bread and put it on a cooling rack.

120   LEMON CAKE BREAD

2 cups almond flour

½ cup coconut flour

½ cup ghee

½ cup coconut oil, melted

½ cup erythritol

4 eggs

2 tbsps. Lemon zest + 1 tsp lemon juice

2 tsp baking powder

Lightly beat eggs before pouring into your bread machine pan. Add in melted coconut oil, ghee, and lemon juice to pan. Add the remaining dry ingredients including blueberries and lemon zest to the bread machine pan.

Set bread machine to quick bread setting.

When the bread is done, remove bread machine pan from the bread machine. Let cool slightly before transferring to a cooling rack.

NUTRITION Kcal: 300 Carbs: 14g Protein: 5g

CHRISTMAS BREAD

Donuts, Holiday Bread

NUTRITION

Kcal: 178
Protein: 4.1 g
Fat: 2.1 g
Carbs: 37 g

35 minutes

3 hours

8 servings

INGREDIENTS

1¼ cups warm whole milk (75°F)

½ tsp lemon juice

2 Tbsp. butter, softened

2 Tbsp. sugar

1½ tsp salt

3 cups bread flour

2 tsp active dry yeast

¾ cup golden raisins

¾ cup raisins

½ cup dried currants

1½ tsp grated lemon zest

Glaze:

½ cup powdered sugar

1½ tsp 2% milk

1 tsp melted butter

¼ tsp vanilla extract

HOW TO MAKE IT

Add each ingredient except the raisins, currants, and lemon zest to the bread machine in the order and at the temperature recommended by your bread machine manufacturer.

Close the lid; select the sweet loaf, low crust setting on your bread machine, and press start.

Just before the final kneading, add the raisins, currants and lemon zest.

When the bread machine has finished baking, remove the bread and put it on a cooling rack.

Combine the glaze ingredients in a bowl and wisk them together untill you have a smoth consistency. Drizzle over once the bread is cooled down.

TEXAS ROADHOUSE ROLLS

Donuts, Holiday Bread

10 minutes   *20 minutes*   *18 rolls*

INGREDIENTS

¼ cup warm water (80°F - 90°F

1 cup warm milk (80°F -90°F)

1 tsp salt

1½ Tbsp. butter + for brushing

1 egg

¼ cup sugar

3½ cups unbleached bread flour

1 envelope dry active yeast

For Texas roadhouse butter:

½ cup sweet, softened salted butter,

1/3 cup confectioners' sugar

1 tsp ground cinnamon

HOW TO MAKE IT

Add each ingredient to the bread machine in the order and at the temperature recommended by your bread machine manufacturer.

Select the DOUGH cycle and press start.

Once cycle is done, transfer your dough onto a lightly floured surface. Roll out the rectangle, fold it in half. Let it rest for 15 minutes.

Cut the roll into 18 squares. Transfer them onto a baking sheet. Bake at 350°F in a preheated oven for 10-15 minutes.

Remove dough from the oven and brush the top with butter. Beat the softened butter with a mixer to make it fluffy. Gradually add the sugar and cinnamon while blending. Mix well.

Take out the rolls; let them cool for 2-3 minutes. Spread them with cinnamon butter on the top while they are warm.

NUTRITION

Kcal: 66
Protein: 4 g
Fat: 3 g
Carbs: 6 g

APPLE PECAN CINNAMON ROLLS

Donuts, Holiday Bread

NUTRITION

Kcal: 190
Protein: 4 g
Fat: 12 g
Carbs: 20 g

 30 minutes

 3 hours

 12 rolls

INGREDIENTS

1 cup warm milk (70°F to 80°F)

2 large eggs

1/3 cup butter, melted

½ cup sugar

1 tsp salt

4½ cups bread flour

2½ tsp bread machine yeast

For the filling:

3 Tbsp. butter, melted

1 cup chopped peeled apples

¾ cup packed brown sugar

1/3 cup chopped pecans

2½ tsp ground cinnamon

For the icing:

1½ cup confectioners' sugar

3/8 cup cream cheese, softened

¼ cup butter, softened

½ tsp vanilla extract

1/8 tsp salt drained

HOW TO MAKE IT

Add each ingredient for the dough to the bread machine in order stipulated by the manufacturer.

Set to DOUGH cycle and press START.

When cycle has completed, place the dough onto a well-floured surface. Roll it into a rectangle. Brush it with butter. Mix the brown sugar, apples, pecans, and cinnamon in a bowl. Spread over the dough evenly.

Beginning from the long side, roll the dough ours cut it into 1¾-inch slices. Transfer them onto a greased baking dish. Cover and let rise for 30 minutes.

Bake at 325°F in a preheated oven for 25-30 minutes. Meanwhile, mix all the icing Ingredients: in a bowl.

Take out the rolls and let them cool. cover warm rolls with the glaze and serve.

CANDIED FRUIT BREAD DELIGHT

Breakfast Bread

10 minutes

3h 30min

9 sevings

NUTRITION

Kcal: 135
Protein: 3 g
Fat: 2 g
Carbs: 26 g

INGREDIENTS

2/3 cup water at 80 degrees F

2 teaspoons melted butter

1 tablespoon sugar

2/3 teaspoon salt

2 cups white bread flour

1 teaspoon instant yeast

1 cup candied fruit

HOW TO MAKE IT

Add all of the ingredients to your bread machine, carefully following the instructions of the manufacturer.

Set your bread machine's program to French bread and the crust type to Light. START the program.

When the cycle is finished and the loaf is done, remove the bucket and allow the bread to cool for 5 minutes.

Shake the bucket gently to remove the loaf and place it on a cooling rack. Cut into slices and serve.

MAPLE SYRUP FLAVORED BREAD

2¼ cups white flour

¼ cup rye flour

1 cup water

1 whole egg, beaten

1 tablespoon melted butter

1 teaspoon salt

1½ tablespoons maple syrup

1 teaspoon dry yeast

Add all of the ingredients to your bread maker and carefully follow the manufacturer's directions. Set your bread machine's program to Basic/White Bread and the crust type to Medium. START the program.

Wait till the cycle is finished. When the loaf is done, remove it from the bucket and set it aside for 5 minutes to cool. Shake the bucket gently to dislodge the loaves.

Transfer to a cooling rack to cool before slicing and serving.

NUTRITION Kcal: 177, Protein: 6 g, Fat: 3 g, Carbs: 33 g

SWEET PUMPKIN SPICE LOAF

Donuts, Holiday Bread

15 minutes   *4 hours*   *12 sevings*

INGREDIENTS

1 1/2 cups all-purpose flour

1 cup canned pumpkin

2 teaspoons baking powder

1 1/2 teaspoon pumpkin pie spice

1 teaspoon vanilla extract, unsweetened

1/2 cup white sugar

1/2 cup brown sugar

1/2 cup chopped walnuts

1/3 cup olive oil

1/4 teaspoon salt

2 eggs, at room temperature

NUTRITION

Kcal: 240
Protein: 4.5 g
Fat: 11 g
Carbs: 33.8 g

HOW TO MAKE IT

In a medium mixing bowl, whisk together the eggs, pumpkin, vanilla, and oil until smooth, then pour into the bread pan.

In a separate medium bowl, combine the flour and other ingredients, and whisk until combined.

Pour this mixture over the egg mixture. Close the lid, then press the "dough" and "start/stop" buttons to knead the ingredients until integrated and coarsely blended.

Choose the "basic/white" cycle option and, if not available, use the up/down arrow buttons to modify the baking duration according to your bread machine model; the baking time will be 2 to 4 hours. If available, press the crust button to pick light or medium crust, then the loaf size, and finally the "start/stop" button to turn on the bread machine.

When the bread machine beeps, open the lid, remove the bread bucket with oven mitts, release the edge of the bread with a nonstick spatula, and tilt the pan over a clean surface to remove the bread.

Allow the bread to cool for 15 minutes on a wire rack before cutting it into twelve slices and serving.

PANETTONE

Donuts, Holiday Bread

15 minutes   *3h 10min*   *14 slices*

INGREDIENTS

¾ cup warm water

6 Tbsp. vegetable oil

1½ tsp salt

4 Tbsp. sugar

2 eggs

3 cups bread flour

1 (¼ ounce) package Fleishman's
yeast

½ cup candied fruit

1/3 cup chopped almonds

½ tsp almond extract

HOW TO MAKE IT

Add each ingredient to the bread machine in the order and at the temperature recommended by your bread machine manufacturer.

Close the lid; select the Sweet loaf, Low Crust setting on your bread machine, and press START.

When the bread machine has finished baking, remove the bread and put it on a cooling rack.

Allow at least one houre before slicing and enjoy fith your family. *Merry Christmas!*

NUTRITION

Kcal: 198
Protein: 4 g
Fat: 6 g
Carbs: 21 g

MEDITERRANEAN BREAD

Mixed Bread

  10 minutes   3h 25min   8 servings

INGREDIENTS

Water – 1 cup

Crumbled feta cheese – 1/3 cup

Garlic cloves – 3, minced

Salt – 1 ¼ tsp.

Honey – 1 tsp.

Olive oil – 1 tbsp.

Bread flour – 3 ¼ cups

Kalamata olive – ½ cup, sliced

Dried oregano – 2 tsp.

Bread machine yeast – ¾ tsp.

HOW TO MAKE IT

Add everything in the bread machine according to bread machine recommendations.

Select Basic cycle and press Start.

Remove the bread when done. Cool, slice, and serve.

NUTRITION

Kcal: 73
Protein: 3 g
Fat: 4 g
Carbs: 8 g

129
THIN CRUST PIZZA DOUGH

Mixed Bread

 10minutes   1h 30min   1 pizza

NUTRITION

Kcal: 156
Protein: 5 g
Fat: 8 g
Carbs: 17 g

INGREDIENTS

Warm water – ¾ cup,

100°F to 110°F

All-purpose flour – 2 cups

Salt – ½ tsp.

White sugar – ¼ tsp.

Active dry yeast – 1 tsp.

HOW TO MAKE IT

Add everything in the bread machine according to bread machine recommendations. Select dough setting and start.

Transfer the dough to a well-floured work surface when done. Roll the dough out into a thin crust and bake.

Take out the bread from the machine and let it cool down completely. Slice the bread and serve.

130
BREAD MACHINE PIZZA DOUGH

Water – 1 ½ cups

Oil – 1 ½ tbsp.

Bread flour – 3 ¾ cups

Sugar – 1 tbsp. plus 1 tsp.

Salt – 1 ½ tsp.

Active dry yeast – 1 ½ tsp.

Add everything in the bread machine according to bread machine recommendations.

Select the Dough cycle.
Remove the dough when done. Roll it out and bake.

Take out the bread from the machine and let it cool down completely. Slice the bread and serve.

ARGENTINE CHIMICHURRI BREAD

Mixed Bread

10 minutes　　　*3h 25min*　　　*15 servings*

INGREDIENTS

Water – 1 cup

White wine vinegar – 1 ½ tbsp.

Olive oil – 3 tbsp.

Cayenne pepper – 1/8 tsp.

Dried oregano – ¾ tsp.

Garlic – 2 cloves, minced

Chopped onion – 3 tbsp.

Fresh parsley – 3 tbsp.

Salt – 1 ½ tsp.

White sugar – 1 tbsp.

Wheat bran – 3 tbsp.

Bread flour – 3 cups

Active dry yeast – 2 tsp.

HOW TO MAKE IT

Place everything in the bread machine according to bread machine recommendations.

Select Basic or White cycle. Press Start.

Remove the bread when done. Cool, slice, and serve.

NUTRITION

Kcal: 32
Protein: 0.4 g
Fat: 2.8 g
Carbs: 1.9 g

MEXICAN SWEETBREAD

Mixed Bread

10 minutes   *3h 25*   *12 servings*

NUTRITION
Kcal: 156
Protein: 5 g
Fat: 8 g
Carbs: 17 g

INGREDIENTS

Milk – 1 cup

Butter – ¼ cup

Egg – 1

Sugar – ¼ cup

Salt – 1 tsp.

Bread flour – 3 cups

Yeast – 1 ½ tsp..

HOW TO MAKE IT

Place all ingredients in the bread machine according to bread machine recommendations.

Select Basic or Sweet cycle. Press Start.

Remove the bread from the machine when it is done and let it cool down completely for about one hour.

Slice the bread and serve.

LOW-SODIUM WHITE BREAD

Water – 1 ¼ cup

Vital wheat gluten – 1 ½ tsp.

White bread flour 3 ¼ cups

Active dry yeast – 2 tsp.

No sodium baking powder – 3 tsp.

Butter – 1 tbsp., unsalted

Oil – 2 tbsp.

Sugar – 2 tbsp.

Add everything according to bread machine recommendations.

Select Basic bread, and Medium crust.

Take out the bread from the machine when fully cooked and let it cool down. Slice the bread and serve.

NUTRITION Kcal: 159, Fat: 3 g, Carbs: 29 g, Protein: 5 g

ITALIAN HERB PIZZA DOUGH

Mixed Bread

10 minutes   1h 30min   15 servings

INGREDIENTS

Warm water – 1 cup

Olive oil – 3 tbsp.

White sugar – 3 tbsp.

Sea salt – 1 tsp.

All-purpose flour – 3 cups

Minced garlic – 1 tsp.

Dried oregano – ¼ tsp.

Dried basil – ¼ tsp.

Ground black pepper – ¼ tsp.

Dried cilantro – ¼ tsp.

Paprika – ¼ tsp.

Active dry yeast – 2 ¼ tsp.

HOW TO MAKE IT

Add everything in the bread machine according to bread machine recommendations.

Select the Dough cycle and press Start. Remove when done.

Allow the dough to rise 30 minutes before using.

NUTRITION

Kcal: 32
Protein: 0.4 g
Fat: 2.8 g
Carbs: 1.9 g

SWEET HO YIN

Mixed Bread

10 minutes　　*1h 20min*　　*15 sevings*

NUTRITION

Kcal: 156
Protein: 5 g
Fat: 8 g
Carbs: 17 g

INGREDIENTS

Lukewarm water 1 ¼ cups

White bread flour 3 cups

Brown sugar ¼ cup

Salt 1 ½ tsp.

Butter 1 tbsp.

Chinese five-spice powder 1 ½ tsp.

Cashews 1/3 cup, chopped

Orange extract 1 ½ tsp.

Active dry yeast 2 tsp.

HOW TO MAKE IT

Combine everything in the bread machine according to bread machine recommendations.

Use the Regular or Rapid bake cycle.

Remove the bread when done.

Cool, slice, and serve.

NO SUGAR-ADDED PIZZA DOUGH

1 cup Warm water (110°F)

Oil – 2 tbsp.

Salt – 1 tsp.

all-purpose flour – 3 cups

Active dry yeast – 1 tbsp.

Add everything in the bread machine according to bread machine recommendations.

Select the Dough setting and press Start.

Transfer the dough on a lightly floured work surface when done. Knead and divide in half.

Make 2 balls and cover with a clean towel. Allow to rise in a warm place for 40 minutes.
Roll out the dough, put tomato sauce & mozzarella. Bake.

NUTRITION Kcal: 820, Protein: 22 g, Fat: 16 g, Carbs: 145 g

GREEK BREAD

Mixed Bread

10 minutes	3h 25min	18 servings

INGREDIENTS

Milk – 1 cup

Crumbled feta cheese – ½ cup

Chopped pitted kalamata olives –

1/3 cup

Water – 2 tbsp.

Oil – 2 tsp.

Bread flour – 3 cups

Sugar – 1 tbsp.

Dried rosemary – 1 tsp., crushed

Salt – ½ tsp.

Active dry yeast – 1 tsp.

NUTRITION

Kcal: 110
Protein: 4.2 g
Fat: 2 g
Carbs: 18.3 g

HOW TO MAKE IT

Add everything in the bread machine according to bread machine recommendations.

Select Basic White bread cycle.

Remove the loaf when done. Cool, slice, and serve.

SEEDED SANDWICH BREAD

Sandwich Bread

15 minutes   *4 hours*   *14 sevings*

INGREDIENTS

For the Bread:

(2 cups) water, boiling

1 tablespoon olive oil

1 ½ teaspoons salt

1 tablespoon brown sugar

3 cups all-purpose flour

1 cup whole-wheat flour

½ cup 7-grain cereal

2 ¼ tsp. bread machine yeast

For the Topping:

1/3 cup chopped dried
cranberries, sweetened

2 teaspoons poppy seeds

2 teaspoons flax seeds

1/3 cup chopped pumpkin seeds

2 teaspoons sesame seeds

HOW TO MAKE IT

Place the two-pound bread recipe in the bread machine after gathering all the ingredients. Combine all the ingredients in the bucket according to the list. Ensure that the yeast does not contain sugar, salt, or wet substances before adding it to the flour.

Create a small well in the middle of the flour and pour the yeast into it.Once the lid is sealed, press the "dough" button and then the "start/stop" button to mix and knead the ingredients.

Combine all the topping ingredients in a small dish and whisk them together. Apply a thin layer of water to the dough's surface, and then evenly distribute the topping ingredients over it.
The bread machine will take 2 to 4 hours to bake, so be sure to select the "basic/white" cycle option and use the up/down arrow buttons to adjust the baking duration according to your model.

The next step is to choose a crust type (light or medium) and loaf size (if available), then press the bread machine's "start/stop" button to make any necessary adjustments.

Once the bread machine beeps, turn it off, put on oven gloves, and remove the bread bucket. Use a nonstick spatula to release the bread from the sides of the pan, and then turn the pan over to remove the bread.

After the bread has cooled for fifteen minutes on a wire rack, slice it into fourteen pieces and serve.

SOFT SANDWICH BREAD

Sandwich Bread

NUTRITION

Kcal: 169
Protein: 6 g
Fat: 1 g
Carbs: 32 g

5 minutes

3 hours

14 sevings

INGREDIENTS

2 Tbsp sugar

1 cup water

1 Tbsp yeast

¼ cup vegetable oil

3 cups white flour

2 tsp salt

HOW TO MAKE IT

Add each ingredient to the bread machine in the order and at the temperature recommended by your bread machine manufacturer.

Make sure the lid is closed, then click the start button on your bread machine after selecting the basic bread, low crust setting.

The bread should be removed from the bread machine and placed on a cooling rack once the baking process has been completed.

HAWAIIAN SANDWICH BREAD

¾ cup pineapple juice

1 egg

2½ Tbsp olive oil

4 level Tbsp sugar

1 tsp kosher salt

3 level cups bread flour

½ cup milk

2 level tsp quick rise yeast

Add each ingredient to the bread machine in the order and at the temperature recommended by your bread machine manufacturer.

Close the lid, select the basic bread, low crust setting on your bread machine and press start.

When the bread machine has finished baking, remove the bread and put it on a cooling rack.

NUTRITION Kcal: 120, Protein: 3 g, Fat: 3 g, Carbs: 21g

MUSTARD RYE SANDWICH BREAD

Sandwich Bread

5 minutes

3 hous

5 sevings

INGREDIENTS

1 cup warm water (110 F)

1/2 cup Dijon-style mustard

2 tbsp. olive oil

1 1/2 tbsp. molasses

2 cups all-purpose flour

2/3 cup rye flour

2/3 cup whole wheat flour

1 1/2 tbsp. vital wheat gluten

2 1/2 tsp. active dry yeast

HOW TO MAKE IT

According to the instructions provided by the manufacturer, place all of the ingredients in the pan of the bread maker machine. Set the machine to either the Basic or White Bread preset, and then start it up.

Remove the bread from the bread machine and placed on a cooling rack once the baking process has been completed. Cut the bread into slices and serve.

NUTRITION Kcal: 163, Protein: 3 g, Fat: 4.5 g, Carbs: 30 g

HONEY WHOLE-WHEAT SANDWICH

4¼ cups whole-wheat flour

½ tsp salt

1½ cups water

¼ cup honey

2 Tbsp olive oil, or melted butter

2¼ tsp bread machine yeast

(1 packet)

Add each ingredient to the bread machine in the order and at the temperature recommended by your bread machine manufacturer. The lid should be closed, the bread machine should be set to the whole wheat, low crust setting, and the start button should be pressed.

The bread should be removed from the bread machine and placed on a cooling rack once the baking process has been completed.

NUTRITION Kcal: 820, Protein: 22 g, Fat: 16 g, Carbs: 145 g

FRENCH HAM BREAD

Meat Bread

10 minutes　　　*3h 25min*　　　*8 servings*

INGREDIENTS

3 1/3 cups of
wheat bread machine flour

1 cup ham, chopped

tbsp. parmesan cheese, grated

½ cup of milk powder

1½ tbsp. sugar

1 tsp. fresh yeast

1 1/3 cups lukewarm water

1 tsp. kosher salt

2 tbsp. extra-virgin olive oil

NUTRITION

Kcal: 280
Protein: 11.4 g
Fat: 5.5 g
Carbs: 47.2 g

HOW TO MAKE IT

Cut the ham into 12 - 1 cm (about 1/4 inch) pieces. Place all of the dry and liquid ingredients in the pan and follow the bread machine directions. Pay close attention to the ingredient measurements. To do so, use a cup, measuring spoon, and kitchen scales.

Set the baking program to French bread, set the crust type to MEDIUM as a result. After the beep, add the ingredients or place them in the bread machine's dispenser. wAdjust the amount of flour and liquid in the recipe if the dough is too thick or too moist.

When the program is finished, remove the pan from the bread machine and let it cool for 5 minutes.

Remove the bread from the pan by shaking it. Use a spatula if needed. Wrap the bread in a kitchen towel and place it in the refrigerator for an hour. Otherwise, make it rest on a wire rack.

CHICKEN CRUST PIZZA

Meat Bread

20 minutes   *2 hour*   *4 sevings*

NUTRITION

Kcal: 186
Protein: 22.4 g
Fat: 10.4 g
Carbs: 2.5 g

INGREDIENTS

Base:

1 pound (450 gr) Ground Chicken

1/4 cup, Grated Parmesan Cheese

1 large egg

Seasonings:

1 teaspoon Garlic Powder

1 teaspoon Onion Powder

1 teaspoon Italian Seasoning

Salt and Pepper to taste

Pizza Toppings:

Pizza Sauce: 1/2 cup

1 Cup Shredded Mozzarella Cheese

Additional toppings as desired

(e.g., pepperoni, bell peppers, onions,)

Bread Machine Complementary Bread Ingredients:

3 cups Bread Flour

1 cup Warm Water (about 110°F)

2 tablespoons, Olive Oil

1 tablespoon sugar

1 teaspoon salt

2 1/4 teaspoons, Active Dry Yeast

Optional Garlic Butter for Bread

(if making garlic knots or breadsticks):

1/4 cup, Butter, melted

2 cloves, garlic, minced

Fresh, chopped parsley for garnish

HOW TO MAKE IT

Prepare the Chicken Crust Manually: Mix ground chicken with seasonings and, if needed, a binding agent like grated Parmesan cheese or an egg. Press this mixture onto a pizza pan or baking sheet, forming your pizza base.

Bake the Chicken Crust: Pre-bake the crust in the oven until it's cooked through and slightly crispy. This step is crucial as it provides the structural integrity for your pizza.

Use the Bread Machine for Complementary Breads: While the chicken crust is baking, you could use your bread machine to prepare dough for garlic knots, breadsticks, or a traditional bread loaf to complement your pizza meal.

Assemble the Pizza: Once the chicken crust is pre-baked, add your favorite pizza toppings - sauce, cheese, vegetables, meats, etc.—and then bake again until the toppings are cooked to your liking.

Serve Together: Present your chicken crust pizza alongside the freshly baked bread from your machine. This combination can offer a delightful contrast of flavors and textures, pleasing to both traditional and adventurous palates.

BREAD WITH BEEF

Meat Bread

20 minutes   *2h*   *6 servings*

INGREDIENTS

5 oz. beef

1 onion

15 oz. almond flour

3 teaspoons dry yeast

5 oz. rye flour

5 tablespoons olive oil

ground black pepper

1 tablespoon sugar

Sea salt

NUTRITION

Kcal: 299
Protein: 13.4 g
Fat: 21 g
Carbs: 6.2 g

HOW TO MAKE IT

Pour the hot water into the 15 oz. wheat and rye flour and let it sit overnight.

Cut the onions and meat into cubes. Fry the onions until clear and golden brown, then add the bacon and cook for 20 minutes on low heat until tender.

Mix the yeast with warm water until smooth, then combine it with the flour, salt, and sugar, kneading thoroughly.

Combine the fried onions, meat, and black pepper in a mixing bowl.

Pour some oil into a bread machine and place the dough inside. Cover with a cloth and let it sit for 1 hour. Close the cover and start the basic/white bread program in the bread maker.

Bake the bread until the crust is medium, then remove it from the oven and let it sit for 1 hour covered with a towel before slicing.

147

CHICKEN BREAD

Meat Bread

10 minutes   *3h 30min*   *1 loaf*

INGREDIENTS

2 cups boiled chicken,

chopped

1 cup lukewarm whole milk

3 cups of wheat bread

machine flour, sifted

1 tbsp. bread machine yeast

1 whole egg

1 tsp. sugar

½ tbsp. sea salt

2 tbsp. extra-virgin olive oil

NUTRITION

Kcal: 283
Protein: 17 g
Fat: 6.3 g
Carbs: 38 g

HOW TO MAKE IT

Pre-cook a chicken leg or fillet and then cut it into small pieces after removing it from the bone.

In a pan, combine all of the dry and wet ingredients (except for the chicken), and bake according to the instructions on the bread machine, paying close attention to ingredient measurements. Use measuring spoons, a cup, and kitchen scales.

Set the baking program to BASIC and the crust type to ME-DIUM.

Once the buzzer sounds, add the chicken or place it in the bread machine's dispenser. If the dough is too dense or moist, adjust the amount of flour and liquid in the recipe.

After the program is complete, remove the pan from the bread machine and allow it to cool for five minutes. Shake the bread out of the pan, using a spatula if necessary.

Wrap the bread in a kitchen towel and refrigerate it for an hour, or place it on a wire rack to cool.

ONION BACON BREAD

Meat Bread

10 minutes   *3 hours*   *1 loaf*

INGREDIENTS

1 cup fried bacon, chopped

3 tsp. bread machine yeast

4½ cups bread machine flour

1 whole egg

1½ cups lukewarm water

1 tbsp. extra-virgin olive oil

3 small onions, chopped

2 tsp. sea salt

2 tbsp. sugar

NUTRITION

Kcal: 391
Protein: 14.7 g
Fat: 9.7 g
Carbs: 59 g

HOW TO MAKE IT

Combine all dry and wet ingredients, except for the additions, in a pan following the bread machine instructions.

Ensure precise measurements by using a measuring cup, spoon, and kitchen scale. Set the baking program to BASIC and the crust type to MEDIUM.

Add the ingredients after the beep or place them in the bread machine's dispenser. If the dough is too dense or moist, adjust the amount of flour and liquid accordingly.

Once the program is complete, allow the pan to cool for five minutes before removing the bread by shaking it out or using a spatula. Wrap the bread in a kitchen towel and refrigerate for an hour or cool on a wire rack.

CHEESE BACON BREAD

Meat Bread

10 minutes   *3h 25min*   *10 slices*

NUTRITION
Kcal: 412
Protein: 16.7 g
Fat: 12.7 g
Carbs: 58 g

INGREDIENTS

7 ounces of diced bacon

4 tbsp. of melted butter

1 1/2 cups of almond flour

1 cup of shredded cheddar cheese

1 tbsp. of baking powder

1/3 cup of sour cream

2 large eggs

HOW TO MAKE IT

In your bread machine, incorporate the following ingredients: flour, baking powder, sour cream, eggs, butter, and cheese.
After selecting White/Basic bread, press the Start button. The dough should be checked after ten minutes, and the bacon should be added after the beep.

When it is finished, remove the bread. After it has cooled down, slice it and serve it.

HAM AND CHEDDAR BREAD

2 eggs

¼ cup beer

2 tbsp. unsalted butter, melted

¼ cup cooked bacon, crumbled

½ cup shredded cheddar cheese

½ tbsp. coconut flour

1 cup almond flour

¼ tsp. salt

½ tbsp. baking powder

Take a bowl and combine the eggs, beer, and butter. Mix the cheese and bacon together until they are barely combined. The bread bucket should be filled with the egg mixture.

Put the flour mixture on top, which is a mixture of flour and dry ingredients, and then cover it. Before pressing the START button, choose between the BASIC/WHITE cycle or the low-carb cycle.
When it is finished, remove the bread. Allow it cool, then slice and serve.

NUTRITION Kcal: 174, Protein: 5 g, Fat: 3 g, Carbs: 31 g

CHILI CHEESE BACON BREAD

10 minutes   *3h 25min*   *10 slices*

INGREDIENTS

¹⁄₂ cup milk

1¹⁄₂ teaspoons melted butter, cooled

1¹⁄₂ tablespoons honey

1¹⁄₂ teaspoons salt

¹⁄₂ cup chopped green chiles

¹⁄₂ cup grated Cheddar cheese

¹⁄₂ cup chopped cooked bacon

3 cups white bread flour

2 teaspoons instant yeast

HOW TO MAKE IT

Preparing the Ingredients. Place the ingredients in your Zojirushi bread machine.

Select the Bake cycle. Set the machine to Regular Basic, select light or medium crust, and press Start.

Remove the bucket from the machine. Let the bread cool for 5 minutes. Gently shake the container to release the loaf and transfer it to a cooling rack.

NUTRITION Kcal: 174, Protein: 5 g, Fat: 3 g, Carbs: 31 g

CONCLUSION

Thanks for making it to the end of this guide.

Bread is considered a fundamental necessity for sustaining life. It is a food that people consume based on personal preference and is widely regarded as a beloved food item. The main ingredients in bread production are flour, yeast, oil, water, salt, sugar, milk, and eggs, with some variation in the process from one nation to another. Bread is a staple at every meal due to its compatibility with a wide variety of cuisines. It is also used to mark special events or celebrate personal achievements. Baking bread at home is simple, requiring basic components such as wheat flour, yeast, salt, and oil, with the option to add sugar, milk, butter, and eggs for enhanced flavor. Using a bread machine can reduce the time and effort needed to knead the dough, making it cost-effective for businesses.

This book presented a wide range of bread recipes for experimentation. Whether sweet or plain, bread is a versatile food that can be enjoyed at any meal. In addition to its delicious taste and versatility, bread also provides essential nutrients such as carbohydrates, protein, fiber, and various vitamins and minerals. It has been a dietary staple for centuries and continues to be a beloved food item in cultures around the world. Whether it's a simple slice of toast for breakfast, a sandwich for lunch, or a side of garlic bread with dinner, bread plays a crucial role in our daily lives. With the rise of artisanal bakeries and specialty breads, the options for enjoying this timeless food are endless.

From today on, you can create your own homemade bread by pressing a few buttons, which means you have the freedom to experiment with your own recipes. If you do, please get in touch; you could be a guest bread chef in my next book.
So roll up your sleeves, and let's get baking!

Camilla

MEASUREMENT & CONVERSIONS

3 teaspoons	1 tablespoon
2 tablespoons	1 ounce
4 tablespoons	¼ cup
8 tablespoons	½ cup
16 tablespoons	1 cup
2 cups	1 pint
4 cups	1 quart
4 quarts	1 gallon

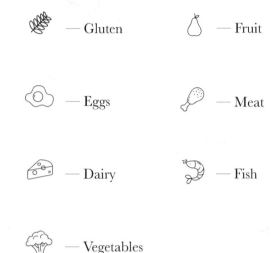

— Gluten

— Fruit

— Eggs

— Meat

— Dairy

— Fish

— Vegetables

Type	Imperial	Imperial	Metric
Weight	1 dry ounce		28g
	1 pound	16 dry ounces	0.45 kg
Volume	1 teaspoon		5 ml
	1 dessert spoon	2 teaspoons	10 ml
	1 tablespoon	3 teaspoons	15 ml
	1 Australian tablespoon	4 teaspoons	20 ml
	1 fluid ounce	2 tablespoons	30 ml
	1 cup	16 tablespoons	240 ml
	1 cup	8 fluid ounces	240 ml
	1 pint	2 cups	470 ml
	1 quart	2 pints	0.95 l
	1 gallon	4 quarts	3.8 l
Length	1 inch		2.54 cm

* Numbers are rounded to the closest equivalent

Gluten-Free – Conversion Tables

All pourpose flour	Rice Flour	Potato Starch	Tapioca	Xanthan Gum
½ cup	1/3 cup	2 tablespoons	1 tablespoon	¼ teaspoon
1 cup	½ cup	3 tablespoons	1 tablespoon	½ teaspoon
¼ cup	¾ cup	1/3 cup	3 tablespoons	2/3 teaspoon
1 ½ cup	1 cup	5 tablespoons	3 tablespoons	2/3 teaspoon
1 ¾ cup	1 ¼ cup	5 tablespoons	3 tablespoons	1 teaspoon
2 cups	1 ½ cup	1/3 cup	1/3 cup	1 teaspoon
2 ½ cups	1 ½ cup	½ cup	¼ cup	1 1/8 teaspoon
2 2/3 cups	2 cups	½ cup	¼ cup	1 ¼ teaspoon
3 cups	2 cups	2/3 cup	1/3 cup	1 ½ cup

Flour: quantity and weight

1 cup = 140 grams
3/4 cup = 105 grams
1/2 cup = 70 grams
1/4 cup = 35 grams

Sugar: quantity and weight

1 cup = 200 grams
3/4 cup = 150 grams
2/3 cup = 135 grams
1/2 cup = 100 grams
1/3 cup = 70 grams
1/4 cup = 50 grams

Powdered Sugar

1 cup = 160 grams
3/4 cup = 120 grams
1/2 cup = 80 grams
1/4 cup = 40 grams

Cream: quantity and weight

1 cup = 250 ml = 235 grams
3/4 cup = 188 ml = 175 grams
1/2 cup = 125 ml = 115 grams
1/4 cup = 63 ml = 60 grams
1 tablespoon = 15 ml = 15 grams

Oven Temperature Equivalent Chart

°F	°C	Gas Mark
220	100	
225	110	1/4
250	120	1/2
275	140	1
300	150	2
325	160	3
350	180	4
375	190	5
400	200	6
425	220	7
450	230	8
475	250	9
500	260	

Butter: quantity and weight

1 cup = 8 ounces = 2 sticks = 16 tablespoons =230 grams
1/2 cup = 4 ounces = 1 stick = 8 tablespoons = 115 grams
¼ cup = 2 ounces = ½ stick = 4 tablespoons= 58 grams

As a heartfelt thank you for purchasing my book, I'm excited to gift you a special holiday recipe bonus, **THE BREAD MACHINE'S HOLIDAY BREADS AND TREATS**, completely for free! Scan the QR code to discover festive, easy-to-make bread machine recipes that bring warmth and seasonal cheer to your kitchen. I hope you enjoy this extra and that it helps make your holiday season truly special!

MAKE A DIFFERENCE IN 60 SECONDS!

One last thing: we'd love to hear your thoughts on this book!

As a small publishing house, your support is invaluable to us. Your feedback can significantly impact everyone involved in bringing this book to life. Sharing how this book has benefited you can make a big difference. I am sure you can imagine how difficult it is for an independent book to collect reviews. Yet, that's one of those little things that are crucial for the survival of a small publishing reality.

If this book has provided you with valuable insights, or knowledge that you've found valuable, your opinion truly matters to us. It's more than just a review; it's a vital support to everyone involved in bringing this book to life.

We take every piece of feedback to heart—in fact, we read every review personally. That is why we would be infinitely grateful if you could spare 60 seconds of your time and leave your genuine opinion.

Use this LINK (https://t.ly/HW23p) or scan the QR code to leave a quick review on Amazon in less than a minute.

For feedback, constructive criticism, questions about the book's content, or request to delve deeper into the book's topics, you can reach out to us at phantapub@gmail.com. Sharing your experience can illuminate the path for future readers and guides us on our journey to create impactful work.

Thank you for your support!